Betty Crocker's

New Choices

for

Two

MACMILLAN • USA

MACMILLAN

A Simon & Schuster Macmillan Company
1633 Broadway
New York, NY 10019-6785

Library of Congress Cataloging-in-Publication Data

Crocker, Betty
[New choices for two]
Betty Crocker's new choices for two.

p.   cm.

Includes index.
ISBN 0-02-860368-0

1. Cookery for two.   I. Title.   II. Title : New choices for two.

TX652.C8318   1995
641.5'61—dc20   95-4980
                                            CIP

10 9 8 7 6 5 4

Manufactured in the United States of America

First Edition

CREDITS

GENERAL MILLS, INC.

Betty Crocker Food and Publications Center

Director: Marcia Copland

Editor: Karen Couné

Recipe Development: Susan Rasmussen

Food Stylists: Kate Courtney Condon and Katie McElvoy

Nutrition Department

Nutritionists: Elyse A. Cohen, M.S., and Nancy Holmes, R.D.

Photographic Services

Photographer: Carolyn Luxmoore

Cover: Iris Jeromnimon

Book Design: Michele Laseau/George McKeon

For consistent baking results, the Betty Crocker Food and
Publications Center recommends Gold Medal flour.

*Cover: Red Beans and Rice (page 76); Back Cover: Curry Chicken Pie (page 106), Cheese Enchiladas (page 86), Fruit Pizza: (page 34);
Title page: Grilled Creole Pork and Peppers (page 52).*

Introduction

Today, more and more households are composed of two people—young couples, roommates, retirees, empty nesters, single parents with a child and various other duos. What do all of these households have in common? The need for tasty, nutritious recipes that are designed just for them. With *Betty Crocker's New Choices for Two*, we've provided just that!

Not only are these tempting recipes perfectly tailored for two, they are also designed to help twosomes eat in a heathy way. Every recipe admirably balances sensible amounts of calories, fat, cholesterol, sodium and, where possible, fiber, and they still taste great! There are easy-to-use symbols indicating recipes especially low in calories, fat, cholesterol and sodium, or high in fiber. For this book, we've added three new healthy categories to the New Choices series: moderate fat—4 to 10 grams of fat per serving; moderate cholesterol—21 to 60 milligrams of cholesterol per serving; and moderate sodium—141 to 360 milligrams of sodium per serving. The new categories provide additional help in reducing fat, cholesterol and sodium in the way that best fits individual eating plans.

These recipes also solve the other problem of cooking for two—new ideas for meals. We've got great recipes for good food all day long. Try Peach Oven Pancake for breakfast, Szechuan Eggplant Linguine for lunch or Chicken Kabobs in Peanut Sauce for dinner, topped off with Fruit Pizza or Cran-Apple Crisp for dessert. There are delicious salads and side dishes, as well as a whole chapter of recipes that let you make two meals from one dish, for even greater convenience and variety.

Let Betty Crocker double your options with recipes that are just right for two, and healthy too!

Betty Crocker

Contents

Nutrition Symbols

Every one of the delicious recipes in this book meets at least one of the five nutritional criteria shown below, may meet several. See page 15 for more details.

 LOW CALORIE

 LOW SODIUM

 MODERATE SODIUM

 LOW FAT

 MODERATE FAT

 LOW CHOLESTEROL

 MODERATE CHOLESTEROL

 HIGH FIBER

Eating Right

Building a Healthy Diet

How can you balance concerns about calories, fat, cholesterol, sodium and fiber and yet still have a food plan that includes foods you love and have eaten all your life? It's actually fairly easy if you take it one step at a time. Approach it as if you're building a house (in a sense, you are—you're building your body for a long, healthy life). Start with a good, solid foundation.

The foundation of a nutritious diet is a wide variety of foods. You need more than 40 different nutrients to maintain good health, and no single food supplies them all in the necessary amounts. And that's just as well because it would be boring eating just one item day after day. Much of the pleasure of food comes from enjoying the flavors and textures of the wonderful assortment of items available to us today.

To best ensure you meet both your nutrient and pleasure requirements, select a wide variety of foods from the Food Guide Pyramid below. Choose low-fat items most of the time, but when you wish, you can occasionally enjoy higher-fat, higher-calorie items, too.

Eat at least the minimum recommended number of servings from each food group daily. Whether you eat more depends on your individual needs.

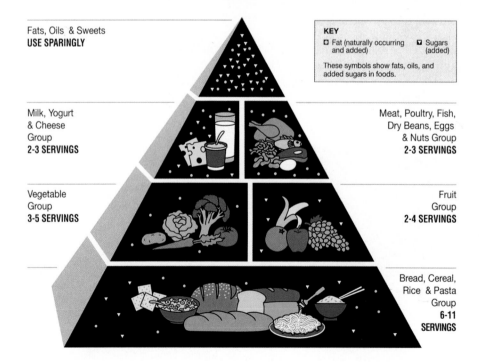

Food Guide Pyramid
A Guide to Daily Food Choices

Fats, Oils & Sweets
USE SPARINGLY

KEY
□ Fat (naturally occurring and added)   ▪ Sugars (added)
These symbols show fats, oils, and added sugars in foods.

Milk, Yogurt & Cheese Group
2-3 SERVINGS

Meat, Poultry, Fish, Dry Beans, Eggs & Nuts Group
2-3 SERVINGS

Vegetable Group
3-5 SERVINGS

Fruit Group
2-4 SERVINGS

Bread, Cereal, Rice & Pasta Group
6-11 SERVINGS

For example, if you exercise regularly, you may require more servings from each group in order to maintain your weight. If you're unsure of how to handle your new food plan, a registered dietitian can help decide what is best for you.

When planning meals, remember the special nutrient concerns discussed earlier. To control fat, saturated fat and cholesterol, select more plant foods, such as cereals, rice, pasta and beans. Use meat, poultry and fish as "flavor enhancers" rather than as the main feature of meals. Use fats and oils sparingly in cooking.

To increase fiber, choose whole-grain cereals and breads, brown rice and dried peas or beans. Serve fruits and vegetables unpeeled. Meet your calcium needs with a wide variety of reduced-fat dairy products. And be wise about sodium by carefully managing the amount of high-sodium foods you eat and how much salt you add to foods during cooking or at the table. Learn to enjoy the natural flavors of foods; enhance flavors with spices and herbs and a small amount of salt only when necessary.

The Framework— A Healthy Attitude

The framework for your healthy body is formed by your attitude about eating and exercise. How you approach making changes, your ideas about weight management and how you manage special eating occasions all combine to make the difference as to whether the changes you first make become permanent changes.

Lasting changes are truly important. Fluctuation back and forth between old and new habits may not only prevent you from ever reaching your goals, but can even cause harm. For instance, constantly losing and regaining weight may end up adding to health problems rather than helping to alleviate them.

As a result, experts today support an approach to improving eating and exercise habits that recognizes individual needs. Gone are the days of preprinted diet and exercise plans. For long-term effectiveness, individual desires, obstacles and issues must be addressed. In short, the approach must be realistic, practical and tailored to each individual. Furthermore, experts advise a slow start to building new habits. If you're a couch potato who skips breakfast and lunch, starts eating the moment you get home from work and doesn't stop until your head hits the pillow, you're not likely to succeed if you try to totally revamp your diet and begin training for marathons at the same time. A better way, and one that is more manageable, is to focus on two or three major eating or exercise habits. For example, you may decide to start eating breakfast and lunch and focus on reducing after-dinner snacking. And you might set a goal for three 20-minute walks a week. When you achieve those goals, you can address other areas you think need improvement. Nothing succeeds better than success, so set yourself up to win by defining small, achievable goals along the way to your overall goal.

Going slowly where weight is concerned is vital, too. The best approach to manage your weight is to eat moderately from the Food Guide Pyramid and exercise regularly. Quick weight-loss schemes, particularly those that advise eliminating any food group, can jeopardize both your nutritional status and your chances for success at weight management.

An effective approach to weight management also considers "healthy" weights. Healthy weights depend on the individual, and for some people, that's far from the superslim fashion model image popular today. Indeed, you may be healthy at a higher weight than your neighbor, even though you both are the same height. A realistic approach allows for a small amount of weight gain, maybe a few extra pounds, as we age.

Two simple measures of healthy weight include determining where excess fat is located (it's considered a greater health risk if fat is found primarily on the abdomen) and if you or your family have a history of health problems that may be aggravated by excess weight, such as diabetes or heart disease. Check to see if your weight falls within a healthy range as defined in the table below.

Suggested Healthy Weights for Adults

Height*	Weight (lbs)**	
	Age 19 to 34 years	Age 35 years and over
5'0"	†97–128	108–138
5'1"	101–132	111–143
5'2"	104–137	115–148
5'3"	107–141	119–152
5'4"	111–146	122–157
5'5"	114–150	126–162
5'6"	118–155	130–167
5'7"	121–160	134–172
5'8"	125–164	138–178
5'9"	129–169	142–183
5'10"	132–174	146–188
5'11"	136–179	151–194
6'0"	140–184	155–199
6'1"	144–189	159–205
6'2"	148–195	164–210
6'3"	152–200	168–216
6'4"	156–205	173–222
6'5"	160–211	177–228
6'6"	164–216	182–234

* Without shoes.

**Without clothes.

† The higher weights in the ranges generally apply to men, who tend to have more muscle and bone; the lower weights more often apply to women, who have less muscle and bone.

Source: *Nutrition and Your Health: Dietary Guidelines for Americans,* Third Edition, 1990, U.S. Department of Agriculture, U.S. Department of Health and Human Services, Washington, D.C.

Being realistic during the food-filled holidays and other special celebrations of our culture is important as well. At those times, it seems that tasty high-fat, high-calorie tidbits lurk in every corner, just waiting to sabotage our efforts. But there's really no need to throw in the towel at these times. You can have your cake and eat it, too. All it takes is a little planning.

It helps tremendously to remember that healthful eating depends on balance, variety and moderation. All foods can fit within a healthful diet; what's important is how often and how much you eat of certain foods. To successfully navigate special occasions anticipate meals high in fat or cholesterol. Offset them by choosing low-fat, low-cholesterol foods the days before and after.

Remember, too, that one mistake does not destroy all your good efforts. If you overeat—for one meal, one day or even one week—you can still salvage your healthful eating efforts by returning to your plan. Compare this behavior with totally giving up because you've made a mistake, and you can see that over time you're more likely to reach your goals. Use the Good Eating Guide (pages 10 and 11) to help you select foods you enjoy that are also healthy. This keeps your eating plan pleasurable and varied.

Finally, any discussion of healthful habits must include a word about exercise. Physical inactivity places more Americans at risk for coronary heart disease—our number one killer today—than any other factor. Although slightly greater risk for the disease comes from cigarette smoking, high blood cholesterol and high blood pressure, the number of Americans who are physically inactive actually exceeds the number who face these other risks. Yet we really don't give exercise the attention it deserves when it comes to its ability to improve and protect our health.

The good news is that we're not necessarily talking about running marathons. Increasing evidence suggests that light to moderate physical activity can have significant health benefits, including a decreased risk of coronary heart disease. For inactive people, even relatively small increases in activity are associated with measurable health benefits. In addition, light to moderate physical activity is more readily adopted and maintained than vigorous physical activity.

As a result, experts today emphasize light to moderate physical activity as the goal for many Americans. Such activity requires sustained, rhythmic muscular movements and is performed at less than 60 percent of maximum heart rate for your age (subtract your age from 220 to get your maximum heart rate). Examples of such activity include walking, swimming, cycling, dancing, gardening, yard work—and even running after young children!

In short, today's advice for adopting healthy lifestyles is to be flexible. A flexible approach to healthy living forms a basic structure that can withstand the assaults of individual strengths and weaknesses. It allows us to live happily and healthfully every day.

Learning the Nutrition Facts

Nutrition Facts is the revised nutrition label that food manufacturers are required by law to use in order to tell us the nutritional content of foods. The hope is that this improved label will be more meaningful to everyone and will enable us to make better food choices.

Nutrition Facts provides much of the same information as the former label with changes in layout and in the emphasis on certain nutrients we want to know more about, namely total fat, calories from fat and total carbohydrate (fiber and sugar). Nutrition Facts is listed for a serving of the food by itself (as packaged), as in dry cereal, and also may be listed for the food plus an added ingredient,

such as cereal plus skim milk, or as prepared, since so many foods require us to cook or add other ingredients before we eat them.

Information about specific nutrients is provided in grams or milligrams per serving "as packaged"; "as prepared" information may be footnoted only. Percent Daily Value, listed for each nutrient, is a measure of how a food stacks up when compared to an average diet of 2,000 calories per day and may be listed for the product as packaged and as prepared. Percent Daily Value replaced the former Percent U.S. RDA for vitamins A and C, calcium and iron. The calories per gram for fat, carbohydrate and protein listed at the bottom of the label enable the reader to calculate the number of calories that come from each component.

Nutrition Facts

Serving Size 1 cup (30g)
Serving Per Container 17

Amount Per Serving	Cereal	with 1/2 cup skim milk
Calories	110	150
Calories from Fat	10	10

	% Daily Value**	
Total Fat 1g*	2%	2%
Saturated Fat 0g	0%	0%
Cholesterol 0mg	0%	1%
Sodium 220mg	9%	12%
Total Carbohydrate 24g	8%	10%
Dietary Fiber 3g	12%	12%
Sugars 4g		
Protein 3g		

Vitamin A	25%	30%
Vitamin C	25%	25%
Calcium	4%	20%
Iron	45%	45%

*Amount in Cereal. A serving of cereal plus skim milk provides 1g fat, less than 5mg cholesterol, 280mg sodium, 30g carbohydrate (10g sugars), and 7g protein.
**Percent Daily Values are based on a 2,000 calorie diet. Your daily values may be higher or lower depending on your calorie needs:

Calories per gram: Fat 9 • Carbohydrate 4 • Protein 4

Good Eating Guide

	Recommended Serving Size	Eat Any Time	Eat in Moderation	Eat Occasionally
Breads/Cereals (6 to 11 servings daily. Includes whole grain, enriched breads and cereals, pasta, rice and crackers.)	1 to 1 1/2 ounces ready-to-eat cereal (varies if it contains fruits, nuts) 1/2 cup cooked cereal, pasta or rice 1 slice bread 1/2 hamburger or hot dog bun 1/2 English muffin or bagel 1 small roll or muffin 1/2 pita (6 inches in diameter) 3 to 4 small or 2 large crackers 2 breadsticks (4×1/2 inch) 1 tortilla (6 inches in diameter) 3 cups popcorn 2 medium cookies	Whole grain* or fortified breakfast cereal Whole grain* or enriched bread, rolls, bagels, English muffins, tortillas, low-fat crackers Brown or enriched white rice Whole grain or enriched pasta Plain popcorn, pretzels and low-fat cookies (such as fig bars) and cake (angel food)	Biscuits Bread stuffing Corn bread Muffins and other quick breads Pancakes, waffles Popcorn made with added fat Taco shells	High-fat crackers Croissants Doughnuts Sweet rolls Snack chips (potato chips, corn chips, etc.) Most cookies and cakes
Fruits/Vegetables (5 to 9 servings daily. Include at least one serving citrus or other choice high in vitamin C daily. Include orange or leafy, dark green vegetables 3 to 4 times a week.)	1 medium fruit such as apple, orange, banana 1/2 grapefruit 3/4 cup juice 1 medium wedge melon 1/2 cup berries 1/4 cup dried fruit 1/2 cup cooked or canned fruit or vegetable 1 medium potato 10 French-fried potatoes (2 to 3 1/2 inches long) 1/2 cup raw chopped vegetables 1 cup leafy raw vegetables, such as spinach 1/8 medium avocado	All fresh, canned or frozen fruits and fruit juices All fresh, canned or frozen vegetables and vegetable juices Plain potato or potato with low-fat topping (such as yogurt)	Vegetables with added butter or margarine Potatoes topped with butter, sour cream or sauces	Fruit pies Deep-fried vegetables French-fried potatoes Vegetables in cream or cheese sauce

Good Eating Guide

	Recommended Serving Size	Eat Any Time	Eat in Moderation	Eat Occasionally
Meats/Protein (2 to 3 servings with a total of about 6 ounces daily. Includes meat, fish, poultry and eggs. Dried beans, peas and nuts are alternatives.)	2 ounces beef (maximum 3 ounces of beef daily) 2 ounces poultry or fish 4 ounces tofu Count the following as 1 ounce of meat: 1 egg (maximum 3 eggs weekly); 3 egg whites; 2 tablespoons peanut butter or whole nuts or seeds; 1/2 cup cooked beans, peas or lentils.	Beef: Lean beef including round, sirloin, chuck and loin Pork: Lean cuts including ham and tenderloin Veal: All trimmed cuts except ground Poultry: All poultry without skin Fish: All fresh and frozen fin fish or shellfish Other: Egg whites, all beans, peas and lentils	Beef: Most cuts including all ground beef, short ribs, corned beef brisket Pork: Most cuts including chops, loin roast Poultry: All poultry with skin Other: Fat-free or low-fat luncheon meats,** peanut butter and other nuts or seeds Eggs: Limit to 3 eggs per week	Beef: USDA prime-grade cuts and heavily marbled cuts Pork: Spareribs, ground pork Lamb: Ground lamb Fish: Fried fish Other: Luncheon meats,** sausages,** frankfurters,** bacon**
Milk/Dairy (2 servings daily. 3 for pregnant or breast-feeding women, 4 for pregnant or breast-feeding teenagers. Includes milk, yogurt, cheese, cottage cheese and pudding.)	1 cup milk 1 cup yogurt 1 1/2 ounces cheese 1 cup pudding 1 1/2 cup ice cream, ice milk or low-fat yogurt 2 cups cottage cheese	Skim milk 1% low-fat milk Low-fat buttermilk** Plain nonfat or low-fat yogurt Low-fat cheeses	2% low–fat milk Part–skim milk cheese** Ice milk	Whole-milk, cream, half-and-half Whole milk yogurt All regular cheese** such as American, Cheddar, Brie, etc. Cream cheese and sour cream

*Good source of fiber.
**For those who need to limit sodium intake, these foods may be high in sodium (read nutrition labels for sodium content).

The Cooking Connection

The way you cook can be just as important as what you choose to cook. For example, a potato baked and topped with nonfat yogurt and chives differs greatly in fat and calories from a potato that's been cut and fried. Other cooking methods, in addition to baking, enable you to use significantly less fat and still prepare a tasty meal. A brief description of some of these cooking methods follows.

- Grill or roast meat on a rack. This allows the fat to drip off instead of pooling around the meat where it can be reabsorbed into the meat.

- Microwave foods. Minimal amounts of added fat or liquid are needed, thereby reducing calories from added fat and minimizing loss of water-soluble vitamins in cooking liquids.

- Pan-broil foods by starting with a cold, ungreased skillet in which meats are cooked slowly. Fat is poured off as it accumulates, before it can be reabsorbed.

- Poach foods by simmering them in a hot liquid just below the boiling point. No added fat is necessary.

- Steam foods in a steamer basket over boiling water. This allows foods such as vegetables to retain their water-soluble vitamins.

- Stir-fry foods in a small amount of oil. Cook uniformly small pieces of food over high heat, stirring constantly. A wok or large skillet is used to stir-fry.

More Ways to Cook Healthy:

- Invest in nonstick cookware.

- Use a nonstick cooking spray.

- Cook onions, garlic or chopped vegetables in water, broth, apple juice, flavored vinegars or wine instead of using oil, butter or margarine to sauté.

- Baste meats with their own juices, broth or vegetable juices instead of oil, margarine or butter; then, make a low-fat sauce or gravy by skimming the fat from the pan juices and reducing the juices by boiling in a skillet.

- Choose herbs and spices, mustard, lemon juice or flavored vinegars instead of butter, oils or salt to spike foods that need a splash of flavor.

- Cut by one-fourth the amount of fat or oil called for in a recipe.

- Try substituting applesauce for half or all of the fat in muffins, cookies and other baked goods.

- Choose low-fat or nonfat versions of dairy products. Most dairy items offer reduced-fat options.

- Use reduced-fat mayonnaise and salad dressings as alternatives to regular products.

- Use purchased fat-free egg substitutes or egg whites instead of whole eggs.

- Add new and unusual greens and other vegetables or cooked beans to salads. These simple additions add fiber and increase vitamins and minerals.

- Limit portions of cooked meat to 2 to 3 ounces per serving by boosting the amounts of vegetables, pasta, rice and beans in chile, soups, stews, stir-fries and casseroles.

- Substitute whole-wheat flour for up to one-half of all-purpose flour in recipes. Foods will be slightly heavier and darker with a heartier texture.

- Decrease or eliminate salt from recipes except for yeast breads, which need salt to prevent excessive rising. Reduce added salt in recipes calling for ingredients that already contain salt, such as chicken broth, tomato sauce or soy sauce. Or choose low- or reduced-sodium versions of those ingredients.

- Do not add salt to the cooking water of rice, pasta or vegetables.

Putting It All Together

The menu plan that follows shows you how to calculate the nutrients in a day's worth of meals. Simply add individual nutrients of the foods you eat during a given day. A sample nutrition profile has been calculated for the day by adding all of the individual nutrients from each recipe or food item eaten. You can then calculate the percent of calories that come from fat. Multiply the number of grams of fat by nine (there are 9 calories per gram of fat) for a total number of calories from fat. (We've done this step for you in our nutrition analysis.) Now, divide the number of fat calories by the total number of calories. That will give you a fraction, which you can change into a percent by multiplying by 100. The equation is:

X Fat Grams × 9 Calories per Fat Gram ÷ Y Total Calories × 100 = % Calories From Fat

Sample Menu Plan

Breakfast

1/2 cup unsweetened strawberries

Sunflower Nut Oven French Toast (page 27)

1 cup low-fat milk

Coffee or tea

Lunch

California Spud Lunch (page 28)

1/2 medium apple

Mango-Lime Cooler (page 44)

Dinner

Hawaiian Broiled Cod with Rice (page 68)

Gingered Carrots (page 120)

Mixed green salad with 1 tablespoon fat-free dressing

12 ounces sparkling water

Cran-Apple Crisp (page 33)

Decaffeinated coffee or tea

Snacks

1 slice cracked wheat toast and 1 tablespoon reduced-fat peanut butter

1 cup Savory Popcorn Mix (page 43)

Nutrition Profile:		% Daily Value:	
Calories	1,850	Vitamin A	100%
Calories from fat	360	Vitamin C	100%
Fat, g	40	Calcium	100%
Saturated, g	14	Iron	100%
Cholesterol, mg	100	**Diet Exchange**	
Sodium, mg	2,110	Starch/bread	
Carbohydrate, g	330	Lean bread	
Dietary Fiber, g	28	Medium-fat	
Protein, g	66	High-fat meat	

Percent fat calculation (using the equation explained above):

40 grams fat × 9 calories/gram = 414 calories

360 calories

1,850 calories = 0.19

0.19 × 100 = 23, or 23 percent calories from fat

If you are not one to count nutrients from each food that you eat, a more general way to track your nutrient intake is to eat the recommended number of servings from the Food Guide Pyramid (page 6). We've listed the number of servings our sample menu provides.

FOOD GUIDE PYRAMID SERVINGS

Breads/Cereals/Rice/Pasta (6–11)	7
Vegetables (3–5)	4.5
Fruits (2–4)	4
Milk/Yogurt/Cheese (2–3)	2
Meats/Beans/Eggs/Nuts (2–3)	2

Nutrition Glossary

Have you been confused by the terms used by nutrition and health experts? Consult this reference list for explanations of some key words.

Additive   Substance added to food to perform certain functions, such as to add color or flavor, prevent spoilage, add nutritional value or improve texture or consistency.

Carbohydrate   Key human energy source. All simple sugars and complex carbohydrates (starches) fit into this category.

CHD (Coronary Heart Disease)   High blood cholesterol levels and buildup of fatlike plaques on the lining of artery walls that limits the flow of blood to body tissues and may cause tissue damage (heart attack in the heart, stroke in the brain) and death. Risk factors include smoking, male gender, family history of CHD, high blood pressure and lack of exercise. Diet, exercise and/or drug treatment are usually warranted. Also called atherosclerosis.

Cholesterol   Essential fatlike substance found in animal foods that is needed by the body for hormones to function properly. Our bodies also make cholesterol.

Daily Values   Set by the Food and Drug Administration as a relative standard for nutrition labeling on foods that are based on the needs of most healthy adults. Percent Daily Values are based on an average diet of 2,000 calories per day. Your daily values may be higher or lower depending on your calorie needs.

Dietary Fiber   Often described as the components of plant foods that are not broken down or absorbed by the human digestive tract. Fiber is a complex carbohydrate based on its chemical structure.

Fat   Provides energy—more than twice the amount supplied by an equal quantity of carbohydrate or protein. Also provides essential nutrients, insulation and protection of body organs.

Food Guide Pyramid   Newly developed nutrition education guide to teach people about foods and the recommended number of servings from each food group to maintain a balanced and healthy diet. It replaces the former Four Basic Food Groups. See page 6 for diagram.

HDL (High-Density Lipoprotein)   This type of cholesterol helps to remove cholesterol from body tissues and blood and return it to the liver to be used again. This recycling process has earned it the reputation of "good" cholesterol.

LDL (Low-Density Lipoprotein)   Often tagged the "bad" cholesterol, low-density lipoprotein cholesterol travels through the bloodstream depositing cholesterol on artery walls and making cholesterol available for cell structures, hormones and nerve coverings.

Minerals   Essential elements other than carbon, hydrogen, oxygen and nitrogen, nutritionally necessary in very small amounts. Minerals are inorganic elements, such as calcium and iron, and are found in our foods and water.

Nutrients   Substances necessary for life and to build, repair and maintain body cells. Nutrients include protein, carbohydrate, fat, water, vitamins and minerals.

Protein   Vital for life and provides energy, structural support of body cells and is important for growth. Made from amino-acid building blocks that contain nitrogen.

Saturated Fat   Primarily found in animal foods, this type of fat is solid at room temperature. Diets high in saturated fats have been linked to higher blood cholesterol levels, but all saturated fats do not have the same blood cholesterol–raising potential.

Unsaturated Fat Found most commonly in plant foods, this type of fat is usually liquid at room temperature. Unsaturated fats may be monounsaturated or polyunsaturated. A laboratory process called hydrogenation is used to alter the chemical structure of unsaturated fats, making them saturated and more shelf stable.

Vitamins Essential substances, found in small amounts in many foods, necessary for controlling body processes. Vitamins, unlike minerals, are organic compounds containing carbon. Vitamins include vitamin A, B vitamins (such as thiamin, niacin, riboflavin) and vitamin C, among others.

Nutrition Symbols

You may find it hard to believe that every one of the delicious recipes in this book meets at least one of the eight nutritional criteria described at right and many meet several. It is unrealistic to expect each dish, or even each meal, to meet all nutritional needs or guidelines. The introduction you just read, "Eating Right," and "Eating for Good Health" (page 132) give you the information you need to use the nutrition analysis provided with each recipe to put together a healthy eating plan for the two of you.

 Low Calorie

Recipes have 350 or fewer calories per serving.

 Low Sodium

Recipes have 140 or fewer milligrams of sodium per serving.

 Moderate Sodium

Recipes have from 141 to 360 milligrams of sodium per serving.

 Low Fat

Recipes have 3 or fewer grams of fat per serving.

 Moderate Fat

Recipes have from 4 to 10 grams of fat per serving.

 Low Cholesterol

Recipes have 20 or fewer milligrams of cholesterol per serving.

 Moderate Cholesterol

Recipes have from 21 to 60 milligrams of cholesterol per

 High Fiber

Recipes have 3 or more grams of fiber per serving.

1

Breakfasts and Snacks

Sunflower Nut Oven French Toast (page 27), Strawberry-Mandarin Smoothie (page 45)

Potato-Egg Skillet

3/4 cup frozen hash brown potatoes with onions and peppers

1 cup fat-free egg product

1/4 cup low-fat milk

3 tablespoons grated reduced-fat Parmesan cheese blend

1 teaspoon chopped fresh or 1/4 teaspoon dried marjoram leaves

Dash of freshly ground pepper

1/4 cup shredded reduced-fat Monterey Jack cheese (1 ounce)

Spray 8-inch nonstick skillet with nonstick cooking spray. Cook potatoes in skillet over medium heat about 5 minutes, stirring frequently, until tender. Mix egg product, milk, Parmesan cheese, marjoram and pepper until blended; pour over potatoes.

As mixture begins to set at bottom and side, gently lift cooked portions with spatula so that thin, uncooked portion can flow to bottom. Cook 3 to 4 minutes, without stirring, or until eggs are thickened throughout but still moist. Sprinkle with Monterey Jack cheese.

1 Serving:		% Daily Value:	
Calories	290	Vitamin A	10%
Calories from fat	125	Vitamin C	6%
Fat, g	14	Calcium	28%
Saturated, g	5	Iron	14%
Cholesterol, mg	15		
Sodium, mg	560		
Carbohydrate, g	23		
Dietary Fiber, g	2		
Protein, g	20		

Mediterranean Eggs

1 teaspoon vegetable oil

3 green onions, chopped (about 1/4 cup)

1 medium tomato, chopped

1 tablespoon chopped fresh or 1 teaspoon dried basil leaves

1 cup fat-free egg product

Freshly ground pepper

Heat oil in 8-inch nonstick skillet over medium heat. Cook onions in oil 2 minutes; stir in tomato and basil. Cook, stirring occasionally, about 1 minute or until tomato is heated through. Pour egg product over tomato mixture.

As mixture begins to set at bottom and side, gently lift cooked portions with spatula so that thin, uncooked portion can flow to bottom. Avoid constant stirring. Cook 3 to 4 minutes or until eggs are thickened throughout but still moist. Sprinkle with pepper.

1 Serving:		% Daily Value:	
Calories	85	Vitamin A	10%
Calories from fat	25	Vitamin C	12%
Fat, g	3	Calcium	6%
Saturated, g	0	Iron	16%
Cholesterol, mg	0		
Sodium, mg	170		
Carbohydrate, g	6		
Dietary Fiber, g	2		
Protein, g	11		

Mediterranean Eggs

Broccoli Egg Bake

Great for an easy breakfast or light lunch, this dish is a good way to use broccoli stems, which are just as nutritious as the flowerets but not as showy. You can also buy broccoli coleslaw if you are on a tight schedule.

1 teaspoon olive or vegetable oil

1 cup broccoli coleslaw blend or broccoli stems, cut into 1 1/4×1/4×1/4-inch pieces

1 large mushroom, chopped (1/4 cup)

2 green onions, chopped

1/8 teaspoon garlic powder

1/2 teaspoon salt

1/2 teaspoon fresh or 1/8 teaspoon dried dill weed

1 tablespoon low-fat milk

1 cup fat-free egg product

1 teaspoon grated reduced-fat Parmesan cheese blend

Heat oven to 375°. Spray 2 tart pans, 4 1/2×1 1/4 inches, or 10-ounce custard cups with nonstick cooking spray. Heat oil in 6-inch nonstick skillet over medium-high heat. Cook broccoli, mushroom and onions in oil until broccoli turns darker green. Stir garlic powder, salt, dill weed, milk and egg product in small bowl until blended.

Spoon vegetables into tart pans. Pour egg mixture over vegetables. Sprinkle with cheese. Place tart pans on baking sheet. Bake 20 to 25 minutes until knife inserted in center comes out clean and edges are lightly browned. Unmold onto plates; serve immediately.

1 Serving:		% Daily Value:	
Calories	90	Vitamin A	10%
Calories from fat	25	Vitamin C	24%
Fat, g	3	Calcium	8%
Saturated, g	1	Iron	16%
Cholesterol, mg	0		
Sodium, mg	730		
Carbohydrate, g	6		
Dietary Fiber, g	2		
Protein, g	12		

Turkey Ham Puffs

2 tablespoons fat-free egg product or 1 egg white

1/8 teaspoon dry mustard

2 tablespoons fat-free mayonnaise or salad dressing

2 slices turkey ham, 1/2 inch thick

Heat oven to 350°. Spray rectangular pan, 10×6×1 1/2 inches, with nonstick cooking spray. Beat egg product and mustard in small bowl on high speed until stiff peaks form; fold mayonnaise into egg mixture. Spread evenly over turkey ham slices; place in pan. Bake 10 minutes or until tops are golden brown.

1 Serving:		% Daily Value:	
Calories	50	Vitamin A	*
Calories from fat	10	Vitamin C	*
Fat, g	1	Calcium	*
Saturated, g	0	Iron	4%
Cholesterol, mg	15		
Sodium, mg	500		
Carbohydrate, g	3		
Dietary Fiber, g	0		
Protein, g	7		

Creamy Vegetable-stuffed Omelet

1 teaspoon fresh or 1/8 teaspoon dried dill weed

1/2 ripe small avocado, peeled and diced

1 medium tomato, diced and drained

1/3 cup fat-free sour cream

1 cup fat-free egg product

Gently stir dill weed, avocado and tomato into sour cream; reserve. Spray 8-inch nonstick skillet with nonstick cooking spray; heat until hot.

Quickly pour 1/2 cup egg product into skillet. Slide skillet back and forth rapidly over heat and, at the same time, quickly stir with fork to spread eggs continuously over bottom of skillet as they thicken. Let stand over heat a few seconds to brown bottom of omelet lightly. (Do not over-cook—omelet will continue to cook after folding.)

Tilt skillet and run fork under edge of omelet, then jerk skillet sharply to loosen from bottom of skillet. Spoon half of sour cream mixture onto center of omelet. Fold portion of omelet nearest you just to center. (Allow for portion of omelet to slide up side of skillet.) Turn omelet onto plate, flipping folded portion of omelet over so far side is on bottom, tuck sides under if necessary.

1 Omelet:		% Daily Value:	
Calories	175	Vitamin A	20%
Calories from fat	80	Vitamin C	12%
Fat, g	9	Calcium	10%
Saturated, g	3	Iron	16%
Cholesterol, mg	15		
Sodium, mg	210		
Carbohydrate, g	13		
Dietary Fiber, g	3		
Protein, g	14		

Potato-Tarragon Scramble

2 large potatoes, cooked and cut into 1/2-inch cubes (about 2 cups)

1 small onion, chopped (about 1/3 cup)

1/2 small red bell pepper, chopped (about 1/4 cup)

1 cup fat-free egg product

2 teaspoons chopped fresh or 1 teaspoon dried tarragon leaves

1/4 teaspoon salt

1/8 teaspoon pepper

Spray 10-inch nonstick skillet with nonstick cooking spray. Cook potatoes, onion and bell pepper in skillet over medium heat about 3 minutes, stirring occasionally, until hot. Mix remaining ingredients; pour into skillet.

As mixture begins to set at bottom and side, gently lift cooked portions with spatula so that thin, uncooked portion can flow to bottom. Avoid constant stirring. Cook 3 to 4 minutes or until eggs are thickened throughout but still moist.

1 Serving:		% Daily Value:	
Calories	195	Vitamin A	16%
Calories from fat	0	Vitamin C	48%
Fat, g	0	Calcium	6%
Saturated, g	0	Iron	16%
Cholesterol, mg	0		
Sodium, mg	440		
Carbohydrate, g	40		
Dietary Fiber, g	5		
Protein, g	14		

Mexican Frittata

1/4 cup instant nonfat dry milk (dry)

1/2 teaspoon chili powder

1/4 teaspoon salt

1 cup fat-free egg product

1 teaspoon vegetable oil

3/4 medium zucchini, shredded (1 cup)

2 green onions, chopped

2 roma (plum) tomatoes, chopped (1/2 cup)

2 tablespoons salsa, if desired

Beat dry milk, chili powder, salt and egg product with hand beater until blended. Spray 10-inch nonstick skillet with nonstick cooking spray. Heat oil in skillet over medium-high heat. Cook zucchini and onions in hot oil, stirring occasionally, about 3 minutes or until crisp-tender. Stir in tomatoes; reduce heat to medium. Pour egg mixture into skillet.

As mixture begins to set at bottom and side, gently lift cooked portions with spatula so that thin, uncooked portion can flow to bottom. Cook 3 to 4 minutes, without stirring, or until eggs are thickened throughout but still moist. Cover; let stand 1 minute until eggs are evenly set. Loosen frittata from pan; carefully slide onto plate. Top with salsa.

1 Serving:		% Daily Value:	
Calories	130	Vitamin A	22%
Calories from fat	25	Vitamin C	20%
Fat, g	3	Calcium	16%
Saturated, g	1	Iron	18%
Cholesterol, mg	2		
Sodium, mg	500		
Carbohydrate, g	14		
Dietary Fiber, g	3		
Protein, g	15		

Peach Oven Pancake

Give this Sunday morning favorite new life throughout the year by using your favorite seasonal fruit.

1/3 cup all-purpose flour

1 teaspoon sugar

1/4 teaspoon salt

1/3 cup low-fat milk

2 eggs

1/2 cup fat-free vanilla yogurt

2 cups fresh or frozen (thawed) peach slices (about 2 medium)

2 tablespoons high-fiber cereal, crushed, if desired

Heat oven to 400°. Spray round nonstick baking pan, 8×1 1/2 inches or 9×1 1/2 inches, with nonstick cooking spray. Heat pan in oven. Beat flour, sugar, salt, milk and eggs with hand beater until smooth. Pour into hot pan.

Bake 15 to 20 minutes or until puffed and browned on edges. Immediately spoon yogurt and peaches into sunken pancake center; sprinkle with cereal. Serve warm.

1 Serving:		% Daily Value:	
Calories	280	Vitamin A	24%
Calories from fat	55	Vitamin C	10%
Fat, g	6	Calcium	16%
Saturated, g	2	Iron	12%
Cholesterol, mg	215		
Sodium, mg	380		
Carbohydrate, g	47		
Dietary Fiber, g	3		
Protein, g	13		

Cinnamon-Orange Breakfast Puffs

4 SERVINGS (3 PUFFS EACH)

If you like, you can also make regular-size muffins. The batter will fill 4 to 5 regular muffin cups. Bake about 20 minutes.

1 tablespoon plus 1 teaspoon sugar

1/4 cup orange juice

2 teaspoons vegetable oil

1/2 teaspoon almond extract

2 tablespoons fat-free egg product or
    1 egg white

2/3 cup all-purpose flour

1 teaspoon baking powder

1/4 teaspoon cinnamon

1/4 teaspoon grated orange peel

3 tablespoons sugar

1/2 teaspoon ground cinnamon

2 teaspoons margarine, melted

Heat oven to 400°. Spray 12 small muffin cups, 1 3/4×1 inch, with nonstick cooking spray. Mix 1 tablespoon plus 1 teaspoon sugar, the orange juice, oil, almond extract and egg product in small bowl until well blended. Add flour, baking powder, 1/4 teaspoon cinnamon and the orange peel; stir just until moistened. Fill muffin cups 3/4 full.

Bake 12 to 15 minutes or until light brown. Remove from pan; cool 5 minutes. Mix 3 tablespoons sugar and 1/2 teaspoon cinnamon in small bowl. Brush each puff with margarine; roll in sugar-cinnamon mixture.

3 Puffs:		% Daily Value:	
Calories	170	Vitamin A	2%
Calories from fat	35	Vitamin C	4%
Fat, g	4	Calcium	8%
Saturated, g	1	Iron	6%
Cholesterol, mg	0		
Sodium, mg	160		
Carbohydrate, g	32		
Dietary Fiber, g	1		
Protein, g	3		

Blueberry Bran Muffins

6 SERVINGS

1/4 cup wheat bran

3 tablespoons honey

2 teaspoons vegetable oil

1/4 cup boiling water

1/2 cup whole wheat or whole wheat blend flour

2 tablespoons quick oats

1 teaspoon baking powder

1/4 teaspoon salt

1/4 teaspoon ground cinnamon

2 tablespoons fat-free egg product or 1 egg white

1/3 cup fresh or frozen (thawed and well drained) blueberries

Heat oven to 400°. Spray 6 medium muffin cups, 2 1/2×1 1/4 inches, with nonstick cooking spray. Stir bran, honey, oil and water in medium bowl until blended. Let stand 2 minutes. Stir in flour, oats, baking powder, salt, cinnamon and egg product until just moistened. Fold in blueberries. Fill muffin cups 2/3 full. Bake 15 to 20 minutes or until golden brown.

1 Muffin:		**% Daily Value:**	
Calories	100	Vitamin A	*
Calories from fat	20	Vitamin C	*
Fat, g	2	Calcium	4%
Saturated, g	0	Iron	4%
Cholesterol, mg	0		
Sodium, mg	180		
Carbohydrate, g	20		
Dietary Fiber, g	2		
Protein, g	3		

Sunflower Nut Oven French Toast

2 SERVINGS (2 SLICES EACH)

This delicious oven French toast is sweetened with frozen apple juice concentrate. Just scoop it out of the can and use it undiluted—it thaws in seconds as you mix it with other ingredients. You can either make juice with the rest of the concentrate, adding a little less water, or keep the container tightly wrapped in your freezer to use in cooking. Photograph on page 16.

1 1/2 teaspoons vegetable oil

2 tablespoons chopped roasted unsalted sunflower nuts

3 tablespoons unsweetened frozen (thawed) apple juice concentrate

1/4 cup fat-free egg product or 2 egg whites

4 slices 12-grain or other multigrain bread

Heat oven to 450°. Spread oil evenly in jelly roll pan, 15 1/2×10 1/2×1 inch, in area the size of 4 slices bread. Sprinkle 2 to 3 teaspoons sunflower nuts evenly over oil. Beat apple juice and egg product with hand beater until blended. Dip bread into egg mixture; place in pan. Drizzle any remaining egg mixture over bread. Sprinkle remaining sunflower nuts evenly over bread. Bake 10 to 13 minutes or until bottoms are golden brown.

2 Slices:		**% Daily Value:**	
Calories	260	Vitamin A	*
Calories from fat	90	Vitamin C	*
Fat, g	10	Calcium	4%
Saturated, g	2	Iron	14%
Cholesterol, mg	3		
Sodium, mg	330		
Carbohydrate, g	36		
Dietary Fiber, g	3		
Protein, g	10		

Veggie Pita Pizza

1 pita bread (6 inches in diameter)

2 roma (plum) tomatoes, chopped (1/2 cup)

1 small zucchini, chopped (about 1 cup)

2 tablespoons chopped onion

1 tablespoon sliced ripe olives

1/2 teaspoon fresh or 1/8 teaspoon dried basil leaves

2 to 4 tablespoons reduced-fat spaghetti sauce or pizza sauce

1/4 cup shredded fat-free mozzarella cheese

Heat oven to 425°. Split bread in half around edge with knife. Place rounds on ungreased cookie sheet. Bake about 5 minutes or just until crisp.

Mix tomatoes, zucchini, onion, olives and basil. Spread spaghetti sauce evenly over rounds. Spoon vegetable mixture over sauce; top with cheese. Bake 5 to 7 minutes or until cheese is melted. Cut into wedges.

1 Serving:		% Daily Value:	
Calories	145	Vitamin A	10%
Calories from fat	20	Vitamin C	20%
Fat, g	2	Calcium	14%
Saturated, g	0	Iron	10%
Cholesterol, mg	5		
Sodium, mg	380		
Carbohydrate, g	26		
Dietary Fiber, g	2		
Protein, g	8		

California Spud Lunch

2 large baking potatoes, such as russets (about 8 ounces each)

1/4 cup reduced-fat sour cream

1/8 teaspoon garlic and pepper seasoning blend

Dash of butter-flavor sprinkles

3/4 cup frozen broccoli, cooked and drained

1 tablespoon chopped red bell pepper

Heat oven to 400°. Prick potatoes with fork. Place in pie plate, 9×1 1/4 inches or 10×1 1/2 inches. Bake 45 to 55 minutes. Slit tops of potatoes and squeeze open. Mix sour cream, seasoning blend and butter-flavor sprinkles. Spoon onto potatoes; top with broccoli and red peppers.

1 Serving:		% Daily Value:	
Calories	170	Vitamin A	10%
Calories from fat	20	Vitamin C	24%
Fat, g	2	Calcium	4%
Saturated, g	1	Iron	4%
Cholesterol, mg	10		
Sodium, mg	45		
Carbohydrate, g	36		
Dietary Fiber, g	3		
Protein, g	5		

California Spud Luch, Mango-Lime Cooler (page 44)

Southwestern Corn Cakes

1 Serving:		% Daily Value:	
Calories	245	Vitamin A	12%
Calories from fat	65	Vitamin C	4%
Fat, g	7	Calcium	18%
Saturated, g	1	Iron	12%
Cholesterol, mg	15		
Sodium, mg	640		
Carbohydrate, g	35		
Dietary Fiber, g	3		
Protein, g	13		

Like a meatless version of this easy breakfast cake? Replace the sausage links with 1/2 cup cooked pinto beans. Photograph on page 25.

1/2 cup frozen (thawed) corn, broccoli and red pepper mixture

1 tablespoon sliced ripe olives

2 cooked reduced-fat pork sausage links (2 ounces), chopped

1 cup low-fat milk

1/4 cup fat-free egg product or 2 egg whites

1/3 cup reduced-fat Bisquick baking mix

2 tablespoons yellow cornmeal

1/2 teaspoon chili powder

1/4 cup reduced-sodium chunky salsa, if desired

Cilantro, if desired

Heat oven to 425°. Spray two 10- to 12-ounce individual casseroles or custard cups with nonstick cooking spray. Spoon half the corn mixture, olives and sausage into each casserole. Place milk, egg product, baking mix, cornmeal and chili powder in blender. Cover and blend on high speed 15 seconds or until smooth. (Or beat on high speed 1 minute.) Pour evenly over sausage mixture.

Bake uncovered 20 to 25 minutes or until knife inserted in center comes out clean. Cool 10 minutes. Top with salsa and cilantro.

Spinach-Bean Tortilla

We have reduced the fat in this colorful Mexican minimeal, but it's still chock-full of fiber, calcium, iron and vitamin C!

1 teaspoon vegetable oil

1/4 cup chopped mushrooms

1 small onion, cut into 1 1/2×1-inch strips

1/2 bag (10-ounce size) fresh spinach, stems removed and shredded (about 3 cups)

1/2 yellow bell pepper, cut into 1×1/2×1/2-inch strips

2 fat-free flour tortillas or whole wheat flour tortillas (8 inches in diameter)

1/4 cup refried beans with roasted chilies

1 small tomato, chopped (1/2 cup)

3/4 cup shredded fat-free Cheddar cheese (3 ounces)

1/4 cup shredded reduced-fat Monterey Jack cheese (1 ounce)

1/4 cup reduced-sodium salsa

Chopped fresh cilantro, if desired

Heat oven to 350°. Heat oil in 10-inch nonstick skillet over medium-high heat. Cook mushrooms, onion, spinach and bell pepper in oil 2 to 3 minutes or until spinach wilts. Place tortillas on ungreased nonstick cookie sheet. Spread beans over tortillas; top with spinach-pepper mixture, tomato, cheeses and salsa.

Bake 10 to 15 minutes or until hot and cheese is melted. Cut each tortilla into 4 wedges; top with cilantro.

1 Serving:		% Daily Value:	
Calories	240	Vitamin A	100%
Calories from fat	45	Vitamin C	68%
Fat, g	5	Calcium	54%
Saturated, g	1	Iron	24%
Cholesterol, mg	20		
Sodium, mg	860		
Carbohydrate, g	33		
Dietary Fiber, g	8		
Protein, g	24		

Swiss Rye Strata

1/4 teaspoon vegetable oil

2 tablespoons chopped onion

4 slices caraway-dill cocktail rye bread, cubed (about 2 cups)

1/2 cup shredded fat-free Swiss cheese (2 ounces)

1/3 cup diced smoked chicken or turkey, if desired

1/2 cup fat-free egg product or 3 egg whites

3/4 cup low-fat milk

1 teaspoon reduced-sodium Worcestershire sauce

1/8 teaspoon pepper

Spray two 16-ounce oval or round individual casseroles with nonstick cooking spray. Heat oil in 10-inch nonstick skillet over medium-high heat. Cook onion in oil, stirring occasionally, about 2 minutes until tender. Mix onion, bread, cheese and chicken; spoon into casseroles. Beat remaining ingredients with hand beater until blended; pour over bread mixture. Cover and refrigerate at least 2 hours but no longer than 24 hours.

Heat oven to 325°. Bake uncovered 30 to 35 minutes or until knife inserted in center comes out clean. Let stand 5 minutes before serving.

1 Serving:		% Daily Value:	
Calories	185	Vitamin A	8%
Calories from fat	25	Vitamin C	*
Fat, g	3	Calcium	48%
Saturated, g	1	Iron	12%
Cholesterol, mg	10		
Sodium, mg	370		
Carbohydrate, g	22		
Dietary Fiber, g	2		
Protein, g	19		

Sweet Pepper Focaccia

Focaccia is an Italian flatbread that looks like a bumpy pizza crust. Keep some in the freezer to make quick lunches and easy snacks. Photograph on page 46.

1 focaccia crust (7 inches in diameter)

1 tablespoon fat-free Italian dressing

1 small green bell pepper, cut into rings

1 roma (plum) tomato, chopped (1/4 cup)

1 teaspoon grated reduced-fat Parmesan cheese blend

Fresh oregano leaves, chopped, if desired

Heat oven to 425°. Place focaccia crust on ungreased cookie sheet; drizzle half of dressing evenly over crust. Top with bell pepper, tomato and cheese. Drizzle with remaining dressing

Bake 5 minutes or until edge of crust is golden brown. Sprinkle with oregano.

1 Serving:		% Daily Value:	
Calories	345	Vitamin A	4%
Calories from fat	100	Vitamin C	26%
Fat, g	11	Calcium	2%
Saturated, g	2	Iron	20%
Cholesterol, mg	0		
Sodium, mg	940		
Carbohydrate, g	57		
Dietary Fiber, g	4		
Protein, g	8		

Peach Bread Pudding

4 SERVINGS

This healthy revision of an old favorite is equally delicious for breakfast or a sweet snack. Make it at sunrise—it will be gone by sunset!

2 cups cubed French bread (about 4 slices, 1/2 inch thick)

2 fresh peaches, peeled and chopped, or 2 cups frozen (thawed) peach slices

1 cup low-fat milk

1/4 cup fat-free egg product

1/4 cup peach or apricot spreadable fruit, melted

2 tablespoons packed brown sugar

1/2 teaspoon vanilla

Peach or apricot spreadable fruit, if desired

Heat oven to 350°. Spray loaf pan, 9×5×3 inches or 8 1/2×4 1/2×2 1/2 inches, with nonstick cooking spray. Arrange bread and peaches evenly in pan. Mix milk, egg product, spreadable fruit, brown sugar and vanilla with whisk or fork in medium bowl until blended. Pour mixture evenly over bread and peaches. Place loaf pan in rectangular baking pan, 10×6×1 1/2 inches, on oven rack. Pour boiling water into pan until 1 inch deep.

Bake 30 to 35 minutes or until knife inserted in center comes out clean. Spread additional spreadable fruit over pudding for glaze. Cool 10 minutes; cut into 4 pieces. Serve warm. Cover and refrigerate any remaining dessert.

1 Serving:		% Daily Value:	
Calories	160	Vitamin A	6%
Calories from fat	20	Vitamin C	4%
Fat, g	2	Calcium	10%
Saturated, g	1	Iron	6%
Cholesterol, mg	4		
Sodium, mg	125		
Carbohydrate, g	33		
Dietary Fiber, g	3		
Protein, g	5		

Raspberry Yogurt Gels

6 tablespoons boiling water

1 1/2 teaspoons sugar-free strawberry-flavored gelatin (1/2 of 4-serving size)

1/2 cup ice water or about 3 ice cubes

1/2 cup frozen (thawed) raspberries with juice

1/2 cup plain fat-free yogurt

Pour boiling water on gelatin in medium bowl; stir until gelatin is dissolved. Add ice water or ice cubes; stir until cubes melt and mixture is cool. Beat gelatin mixture, raspberries and yogurt in medium bowl at medium speed until blended. Pour into two 1-cup serving dishes. Cover and refrigerate at least 30 minutes or until set.

1 Serving:		% Daily Value:	
Calories	90	Vitamin A	*
Calories from fat	0	Vitamin C	18%
Fat, g	0	Calcium	12%
Saturated, g	0	Iron	2%
Cholesterol, mg	0		
Sodium, mg	50		
Carbohydrate, g	21		
Dietary Fiber, g	2		
Protein, g	4		

Cran-Apple Crisp

Apples are always readily available, regardless of the season. The best varieties for baking are Braeburn, Fuji, Gala, Golden Delicious, Granny Smith, Greening, Haralson, Jonagold, Newton Pippin, Prairie Spy and San Rose. Try them all!

2 baking apples, cored and sliced

1 teaspoon lemon juice

1 tablespoon dried cranberries

1 tablespoon packed brown sugar

1 tablespoon margarine, melted

4 gingersnaps, crushed

Heat oven to 375°. Spray 1-quart casserole with nonstick cooking spray. Place apples in dish; sprinkle with lemon juice. Mix remaining ingredients until crumbly; sprinkle over apples. Cover with aluminum foil. Bake 30 to 40 minutes or until apples are tender.

1 Serving:		% Daily Value:	
Calories	225	Vitamin A	8%
Calories from fat	70	Vitamin C	8%
Fat, g	8	Calcium	2%
Saturated, g	2	Iron	4%
Cholesterol, mg	0		
Sodium, mg	150		
Carbohydrate, g	40		
Dietary Fiber, g	3		
Protein, g	1		

Granola Candy

12 CANDIES

1/2 cup fat-free or low-fat granola

1/2 cup multigrain puffed cereal

2 tablespoons raisins or dried cranberries, if desired

1/2 cup miniature marshmallows

1 tablespoon honey

1 tablespoon reduced-fat peanut butter

Mix granola, puffed cereal and raisins in medium bowl. Heat remaining ingredients in small nonstick saucepan over low heat, stirring constantly, until marshmallows are melted. Immediately pour marshmallow mixture over cereal mixture; stir until coated. With wet hands, divide into 1 1/2-inch balls. Place on waxed paper. Refrigerate at least 10 minutes.

1 Candy:		% Daily Value:	
Calories	50	Vitamin A	*
Calories from fat	10	Vitamin C	*
Fat, g	1	Calcium	*
Saturated, g	0	Iron	*
Cholesterol, mg	0		
Sodium, mg	10		
Carbohydrate, g	9		
Dietary Fiber, g	0		
Protein, g	1		

Fruit Pizza

1 fat-free flour or whole wheat flour tortilla (8 inches in diameter)

1/2 teaspoon sugar

Dash cinnamon

2 tablespoons fat-free soft cream cheese

1/2 cup chopped fresh fruit (such as strawberries, grapes, peaches), well drained

Heat oven to 350°. Place tortilla on ungreased cookie sheet. Bake about 10 minutes or until crisp. Meanwhile, mix sugar and cinnamon; reserve. Place hot tortilla on cutting board; spread cream cheese on tortilla. Sprinkle with sugar-cinnamon mixture; arrange fruit on top. Cut into 4 wedges; serve warm.

1 Serving:		% Daily Value:	
Calories	50	Vitamin A	*
Calories from fat	0	Vitamin C	20%
Fat, g	0	Calcium	2%
Saturated, g	0	Iron	4%
Cholesterol, mg	0		
Sodium, mg	165		
Carbohydrate, g	12		
Dietary Fiber, g	2		
Protein, g	3		

Fruit Pizza

Hot Artichoke Appetizer

2 SERVINGS (6 APPETIZERS EACH)

You'll love this lower-fat version of the popular hot appetizer spread. Serve it on crackers to warm up chilly fall and winter evenings.

1/4 package (10-ounce size) frozen artichokes, partially thawed

1/4 cup water

1 tablespoon finely chopped red bell pepper

1/2 teaspoon dry nonfat Italian salad dressing mix (dry)

1/2 cup fat-free mayonnaise or salad dressing

2 green onions, chopped

12 reduced-fat crackers

Heat artichokes in water in 1-quart saucepan over medium heat 5 to 8 minutes, breaking up chunks and stirring occasionally, until artichokes are completely thawed; drain. Chop artichokes; place in saucepan. Stir in remaining ingredients except crackers. Cook over low heat 1 to 2 minutes, stirring constantly, until well blended and hot. Spoon onto crackers.

6 Appetizers:		% Daily Value:	
Calories	160	Vitamin A	4%
Calories from fat	35	Vitamin C	12%
Fat, g	4	Calcium	4%
Saturated, g	1	Iron	8%
Cholesterol, mg	0		
Sodium, mg	1,060		
Carbohydrate, g	30		
Dietary Fiber, g	2		
Protein, g	3		

Zucchini Snackers

2 SERVINGS (6 APPETIZERS EACH)

1 medium zucchini (about 1 1/2 inches in diameter)

1/4 cup finely chopped red bell pepper

2 tablespoons chopped fresh parsley

1/2 teaspoon onion and herb seasoning mix

1/3 cup fat-free soft cream cheese

2 drops red pepper sauce

Cut zucchini lengthwise into 6 strips. Cut each strip in half crosswise; trim each piece to 2 inches. Mix remaining ingredients. Spoon 2 to 3 teaspoons red pepper spread on each piece of zucchini.

6 Appetizers:		% Daily Value:	
Calories	50	Vitamin A	14%
Calories from fat	0	Vitamin C	62%
Fat, g	0	Calcium	6%
Saturated, g	0	Iron	4%
Cholesterol, mg	0		
Sodium, mg	240		
Carbohydrate, g	6		
Dietary Fiber, g	1		
Protein, g	7		

BONING UP ON CALCIUM

Loss of bone mass is a natural process of aging and after about age 35, you cannot add to bone density. But you can take steps to help preserve the bone mass that you have by eating calcium-rich foods along with vitamin D and exercising regularly. Here are some ideas for increasing calcium consumption:

- Stir one of these easy-to-prepare combinations into fat-free cottage cheese for a snack: shredded carrots and raisins; crushed pineapple and fresh mint; chopped green bell pepper, tomato and onion; sunflower nuts, alfalfa sprouts and chopped carrots; or toasted pine nuts, chopped tomato and basil.

- Mix preserves or jam into fat-free cottage cheese or cream cheese. Spread on bagels or English muffins and broil.

- Eat ice milk or fat-free yogurt for dessert.

- Drink calcium-fortified juices instead of soft drinks.

- Snack on raw broccoli or other vegetables that are good sources of calcium like kale, collards and spinach.

- Don't discard the soft bones of canned fish such as sardines or salmon—they contain significant amounts of calcium.

Mediterranean Bean and Basil Spread

4 SERVINGS

If you don't have access to fresh basil, look for the convenient jarred minced basil in water—it's available at most supermarkets. This enticing spread is delicious on Baked Pita Chips (page 42).

1 cup garbanzo beans, rinsed and drained

1/4 cup fat-free Italian dressing

1/3 cup fresh basil leaves or 2 tablespoons minced basil in water

1/2 teaspoon garlic powder

Reduced-sodium salt, if desired

Place all ingredients in blender or food processor. Cover and blend at medium-high speed, stopping blender occasionally to scrape sides, until smooth. Salt to taste.

1 Serving:		% Daily Value:	
Calories	55	Vitamin A	2%
Calories from fat	0	Vitamin C	2%
Fat, g	0	Calcium	2%
Saturated, g	0	Iron	8%
Cholesterol, mg	0		
Sodium, mg	220		
Carbohydrate, g	12		
Dietary Fiber, g	2		
Protein, g	4		

Pepperoncini Spread

Pepperoncini are pickled salad peppers—the kind that Peter Piper picked in the famous tongue twister! They are salty, so serve them with low-sodium accompaniments and a thirst-quenching drink, such as lemonade. Try serving the spread with vegetable sticks, crackers or Baked Pita Chips (page 42).

2 sun-dried tomato halves (not oil-packed)

Boiling water

1/2 cup fat-free sour cream

1 tablespoon low-fat milk

1 tablespoon grated reduced-fat Parmesan cheese blend

6 pepperoncini, drained and stemmed

4 ripe olives, chopped

Cover tomato halves with boiling water; let stand 5 minutes. Drain and chop. Place sour cream, milk, cheese and pepperoncini in blender or food processor. Cover and blend 1 minute, stopping occasionally to scrape sides. Blend 1 minute longer or until smooth. Place in small bowl; stir in tomato and olives.

1 Serving:		% Daily Value:	
Calories	95	Vitamin A	26%
Calories from fat	10	Vitamin C	100%
Fat, g	1	Calcium	14%
Saturated, g	0	Iron	4%
Cholesterol, mg	5		
Sodium, mg	290		
Carbohydrate, g	16		
Dietary Fiber, g	1		
Protein, g	6		

Maple-Nut Cheese Spread

This not-too-sweet spread is equally good on low-fat crackers or sliced apples and pears.

1/4 cup fat-free cream cheese, softened

2 teaspoons reduced-calorie maple-flavored syrup

2 teaspoons chopped walnuts

1 drop maple flavoring, if desired

Mix all ingredients until blended.

1 Serving:		% Daily Value:	
Calories	45	Vitamin A	2%
Calories from fat	15	Vitamin C	0%
Fat, g	2	Calcium	2%
Saturated, g	0	Iron	0%
Cholesterol, mg	0		
Sodium, mg	190		
Carbohydrate, g	3		
Dietary Fiber, g	0		
Protein, g	4		

Pepperoncini Spread, Maple-Nut Cheese Spread, Savory Popcorn Mix (page 43), Oriental Crisps (page 42), Baked Pita Chips (page 42)

Almost Guacamole

3 SERVINGS

You absolutely won't miss the fat in this lower-fat version of guacamole! And it won't darken when it sits out. To keep the unused half of the avocado from darkening, rub lemon juice on the cut edge and cover tightly with plastic wrap. Store in the refrigerator. Use the remaining avocado for Chicken and Avocado with Sweet Pepper Sauce (page 60).

2 sun-dried tomato halves (not oil-packed)

Boiling water

1/3 cup frozen (thawed) peas

1/4 cup fat-free mayonnaise or salad dressing

1/8 teaspoon salt

Dash of pepper

1 tablespoon lemon juice

1/4 cup coarsely chopped onion

1/2 medium ripe avocado, cut into chunks

12 fresh cilantro leaves, if desired

Cover tomato halves with boiling water; let stand 5 minutes. Drain and chop. Place peas, mayonnaise, salt, pepper, lemon juice and onion in blender or food processor. Cover and blend at medium-high speed, stopping blender occasionally to scrape sides, until smooth. Add avocado and cilantro; blend until smooth. Place in small bowl; stir in tomato.

1 Serving:		% Daily Value:	
Calories	95	Vitamin A	2%
Calories from fat	45	Vitamin C	10%
Fat, g	5	Calcium	*
Saturated, g	1	Iron	4%
Cholesterol, mg	0		
Sodium, mg	470		
Carbohydrate, g	12		
Dietary Fiber, g	2		
Protein, g	2		

Curried Jicama Dip

Jicama is a crunchy southwestern root vegetable. It's available November through May in most large supermarkets, Mexican specialty stores and farmers markets. Cut the desired amount from the root and peel off the brown skin just before use. Store the remaining root tightly wrapped in the refrigerator up to about 1 week. For a crunchy snack, serve the dip with vegetables or low-fat crackers.

1 teaspoon olive oil

2 tablespoons coarsely chopped onion

1 clove garlic, chopped

1/2 teaspoon curry powder

1/4 teaspoon ground cumin

1/4 cup shredded jicama

1/4 cup frozen (thawed) corn with red peppers

1/4 cup fat-free mayonnaise or salad dressing

1/2 teaspoon lime juice

Heat oil in 10-inch skillet over medium heat. Cook onion and garlic in oil, stirring constantly, 2 minutes or until onions are soft and golden. Remove from heat. Immediately add curry powder and cumin to hot onion mixture; stir 1 minute. Spoon onion mixture into medium bowl. Stir in remaining ingredients until blended.

1 Serving:		% Daily Value:	
Calories	70	Vitamin A	*
Calories from fat	20	Vitamin C	8%
Fat, g	2	Calcium	*
Saturated, g	0	Iron	2%
Cholesterol, mg	0		
Sodium, mg	390		
Carbohydrate, g	13		
Dietary Fiber, g	1		
Protein, g	1		

Tomatillo Dip

3 SERVINGS

1/2 cup water

1/4 teaspoon salt

1/8 teaspoon ground cumin

1/8 teaspoon pepper

1-inch fresh Anaheim chile, seeds and ribs removed and coarsely chopped

1/2- to 1-inch fresh hot red jalapeño chile, coarsely chopped, if desired

2 green onions, coarsely chopped

1/2 pound tomatillos (6 or 7), husked, washed and quartered

2 tablespoons fresh cilantro leaves, loosely packed

Place all ingredients except cilantro in 1-quart saucepan. Cover and cook over medium heat 12 to 15 minutes, stirring occasionally, until tomatillos are soft. Cool 15 minutes. Place in blender or food processor. Add cilantro. Cover and blend at medium-high speed, stopping blender occasionally to scrape sides, until smooth. Refrigerate at least 1 hour or until chilled.

Green Tomato Dip: Substitute 1 large green tomato, chopped, and 1 teaspoon lime juice for the tomatillos.

1 Serving:		% Daily Value:	
Calories	20	Vitamin A	18%
Calories from fat	0	Vitamin C	36%
Fat, g	0	Calcium	2%
Saturated, g	0	Iron	4%
Cholesterol, mg	0		
Sodium, mg	190		
Carbohydrate, g	5		
Dietary Fiber, g	1		
Protein, g	1		

DON'T DESERT DESSERT

You don't have to give up dessert in a healthful eating plan. And you can even enjoy some of your rich favorites occasionally. For more frequent sampling, however, there are lots of light and tasty treats you can eat. Here are a few suggestions:

- Sliced strawberries topped with a mixture of reduced-fat whipped topping and finely chopped fresh mint leaves.

- Sliced peaches topped with fat-free raspberry yogurt and low-fat granola.

- Seedless green grapes topped with fat-free vanilla yogurt and a little brown sugar.

- Fresh pineapple slice drizzled with rum or apple juice and sprinkled with finely chopped crystallized ginger and toasted shredded coconut.

- Angel food cake topped with fat-free lemon yogurt and fresh raspberries.

- Gingersnaps spread with fat-free cream cheese.

- Vanilla ice milk topped with reduced-calorie maple-flavored syrup and low-fat granola.

- Orange frozen yogurt topped with crumbled gingersnaps.

Oriental Crisps

4 SERVINGS (12 CRISPS EACH)

Here's a delightful alternative to fried tortilla chips! These crunchy baked triangles of wonton wrappers make for a surefire snack. Photograph on page 39.

24 wonton wrappers

1/2 teaspoon garlic powder

1 teaspoon fat-free egg product or egg white

1 teaspoon reduced-sodium soy sauce

Heat oven to 375°. Spray 2 cookie sheets with nonstick cooking spray. Cut wonton wrappers diagonally to form triangles. Beat garlic powder, egg product and soy sauce with a fork until thoroughly blended. Brush triangles with egg mixture. Place 1/2 inch apart on cookie sheets. Bake cookie sheets, one at a time, 5 minutes until wonton wrappers are brown and crisp. Immediately remove from cookie sheet; cool on wire rack.

Salted Crisps: Omit garlic powder and soy sauce. Thin egg with a few drops water. Brush triangles with egg mixture. Sprinkle 1/4 teaspoon reduced-sodium light salt on triangles. Continue as directed.

Parmesan Crisps: Omit garlic powder and soy sauce. Thin egg with a few drops water. Brush triangles with egg mixture. Sprinkle 1/2 teaspoon grated reduced-fat Parmesan cheese blend on triangles. Continue as directed.

Onion-Herb Crisps: Omit garlic powder and soy sauce. Thin egg with a few drops water. Brush triangles with egg mixture. Sprinkle 1/2 teaspoon onion and herb seasoning blend on triangles. Continue as directed.

12 Crisps:		% Daily Value:	
Calories	225	Vitamin A	*
Calories from fat	10	Vitamin C	*
Fat, g	1	Calcium	10%
Saturated, g	0	Iron	16%
Cholesterol, mg	0		
Sodium, mg	460		
Carbohydrate, g	48		
Dietary Fiber, g	2		
Protein, g	8		

Baked Pita Chips

4 SERVINGS (8 CHIPS EACH)

Photograph on page 39.

2 whole wheat pita breads (6 inches in diameter)

Heat oven to 400°. Split pita breads in half around edge with knife. Cut each half into 8 wedges. Place in single layer on ungreased cookie sheet. Bake about 9 minutes or until crisp and light brown; cool.

8 Chips:		% Daily Value:	
Calories	80	Vitamin A	*
Calories from fat	10	Vitamin C	*
Fat, g	1	Calcium	*
Saturated, g	0	Iron	4%
Cholesterol, mg	0		
Sodium, mg	160		
Carbohydrate, g	17		
Dietary Fiber, g	2		
Protein, g	3		

Dilly Oyster Crackers

4 SERVINGS (1/3 CUP EACH)

1 tablespoon grated reduced-fat Parmesan cheese blend

1/2 teaspoon garlic powder

1 1/2 teaspoons fresh or 1/2 teaspoon dried dill weed

1 tablespoon water

1 1/3 cups oyster crackers

Heat oven to 300°. Spray jelly roll pan, 15×10 1/2×1/2 inch, with nonstick cooking spray. Mix cheese blend, garlic powder, dill weed and water in medium bowl. Quickly toss crackers in seasoning mixture with slotted spoon; spread in pan.

Bake 6 to 8 minutes, stirring and turning twice, until lightly browned and dry to the touch. Pour into serving bowl. Stir once as crackers cool.

Herb Crackers: Substitute 2 teaspoons onion and herb seasonings blend for the Parmesan cheese blend, garlic powder and dill weed.

Chili Crackers: Substitute 1/2 teaspoon chili powder for the Parmesan cheese blend and dill weed.

1/3 Cup:		% Daily Value:	
Calories	55	Vitamin A	*
Calories from fat	10	Vitamin C	*
Fat, g	1	Calcium	2%
Saturated, g	0	Iron	2%
Cholesterol, mg	0		
Sodium, mg	190		
Carbohydrate, g	10		
Dietary Fiber, g	0		
Protein, g	2		

Savory Popcorn Mix

4 SERVINGS (ABOUT 1 CUP EACH)

Photograph on page 39.

3 cups hot-air-popped popcorn

1 cup pretzel sticks

1 cup tiny fish-shaped crackers

1 tablespoon margarine, melted

1/4 teaspoon garlic powder

1/4 teaspoon onion powder

1/4 teaspoon dried oregano leaves

1/4 teaspoon dried basil leaves

1 to 3 drops red pepper sauce

Heat oven to 300°. Mix popcorn, pretzel sticks and crackers in rectangular pan, 13×9×2 inches. Mix remaining ingredients. Drizzle over popcorn mixture; toss until evenly coated. Bake, stirring every 10 minutes, until toasted, about 30 minutes. Serve warm.

1 Cup:		% Daily Value:	
Calories	155	Vitamin A	4%
Calories from fat	65	Vitamin C	*
Fat, g	7	Calcium	2%
Saturated, g	2	Iron	6%
Cholesterol, mg	2		
Sodium, mg	360		
Carbohydrate, g	21		
Dietary Fiber, g	1		
Protein, g	3		

Mango-Lime Cooler

Photograph on page 29.

1 ripe mango, peeled and cut into chunks
1/2 cup plain fat-free yogurt
1/2 cup low-fat milk
1 tablespoon honey
1 tablespoon lime juice
3 ice cubes, crushed

Place all ingredients except ice cubes in blender. Cover and blend on high speed about 15 seconds or until smooth. Add crushed ice and continue blending for 15 seconds or until blended.

1 Serving:		% Daily Value:	
Calories	165	Vitamin A	44%
Calories from fat	20	Vitamin C	52%
Fat, g	2	Calcium	20%
Saturated, g	1	Iron	2%
Cholesterol, mg	5		
Sodium, mg	80		
Carbohydrate, g	34		
Dietary Fiber, g	3		
Protein, g	6		

Pineapple-Lemon Frost

1 can (6 ounces) unsweetened pineapple juice
1/2 pint lemon sorbet (1 cup)
Mint leaves, if desired

Place pineapple juice and lemon sorbet in blender. Cover and blend until smooth. Pour into two 8-ounce glasses. Garnish with mint leaves. Serve immediately.

1 Serving:		% Daily Value:	
Calories	185	Vitamin A	*
Calories from fat	0	Vitamin C	48%
Fat, g	0	Calcium	2%
Saturated, g	0	Iron	2%
Cholesterol, mg	0		
Sodium, mg	20		
Carbohydrate, g	45		
Dietary Fiber, g	0		
Protein, g	1		

Strawberry-Mandarin Smoothie

Photograph on page 16.

1 1/4 cups sliced fresh or frozen (thawed) strawberries (8 ounces)

1/3 cup frozen (thawed) mandarin tangerine juice concentrate*

1/2 cup fat-free vanilla yogurt

1/3 cup cold water

2 strawberries with leaves, if desired

Place 1 1/4 cups sliced strawberries, juice concentrate, yogurt and water in blender. Cover and blend on medium-high speed until smooth. Pour into two 8-ounce glasses. Make a slit in strawberries; place on rim of glasses as garnish.

*Frozen orange juice concentrate may be substituted for the mandarin tangerine juice concentrate.

1 Serving:		% Daily Value:	
Calories	130	Vitamin A	2%
Calories from fat	0	Vitamin C	100%
Fat, g	0	Calcium	14%
Saturated, g	0	Iron	2%
Cholesterol, mg	0		
Sodium, mg	50		
Carbohydrate, g	30		
Dietary Fiber, g	2		
Protein, g	5		

2

Main Dishes

*Chicken Kabobs in
Peanut Sauce (page
58), Sweet Pepper
Focaccia (page 32)*

Spicy Beef Stir-fry

Feeling hungry? Then this is the recipe for you! We have managed to double the amount of rice you can eat yet keep the calories well under that of a traditional beef stir-fry. And as a bonus, say good-bye to about 15 grams of fat!

2 teaspoons soy sauce

2 teaspoons cornstarch

1 to 2 teaspoons Chinese chili sauce with garlic

1 teaspoon sesame or vegetable oil

1/2 pound beef flank steak, cut across grain into 1/8-inch strips

1 teaspoon sesame or vegetable oil

1 medium summer squash, cut into 1/4-inch slices (1 1/2 cups)

1/2 cup reduced-sodium chicken broth

1/3 pound Chinese pea pods, cut diagonally into pieces (1 cup)

2 cups hot cooked rice or soba noodles

Mix soy sauce, cornstarch and chili sauce; reserve. Heat wok or 10-inch nonstick skillet until 1 to 2 drops water bubble and skitter when sprinkled in wok. Add 1 teaspoon oil and rotate wok to coat bottom and side. Add beef. Stir-fry 2 to 3 minutes or until beef is brown; remove from wok.

Add 1 teaspoon oil and rotate wok to coat side. Add squash. Stir-fry 1 minute. Add broth; cover and reduce heat to low. Cook 3 minutes or until squash is tender. Stir in cornstarch mixture, pea pods and beef. Stir-fry over high heat 2 minutes or until pea pods are crisp-tender. Serve over rice.

1 Serving:		% Daily Value:	
Calories	455	Vitamin A	44%
Calories from fat	115	Vitamin C	34%
Fat, g	13	Calcium	6%
Saturated, g	4	Iron	32%
Cholesterol, mg	60		
Sodium, mg	540		
Carbohydrate, g	56		
Dietary Fiber, g	3		
Protein, g	31		

Italian Meatballs

1/2 pound extra-lean ground beef

3 tablespoons Italian-style dry bread crumbs

1/2 teaspoon chopped fresh or 1/4 teaspoon dried oregano leaves

2 tablespoons fat-free egg product or 1 egg white

1/4 cup pizza sauce

Heat oven to 375°. Mix ground beef, bread crumbs, oregano and egg white. Shape mixture into 8 meatballs. Place in ungreased square pan, 8×8×2 inches. Bake about 20 minutes or until meatballs are no longer pink in center. Spoon pizza sauce over meatballs. Bake 2 minutes longer.

1 Serving:		% Daily Value:	
Calories	255	Vitamin A	2%
Calories from fat	115	Vitamin C	4%
Fat, g	13	Calcium	4%
Saturated, g	5	Iron	18%
Cholesterol, mg	70		
Sodium, mg	300		
Carbohydrate, g	10		
Dietary Fiber, g	1		
Protein, g	26		

Cajun Beef and Rice

A little meat goes a long way in this hearty main dish. Okra does double duty here; it adds wonderful flavor and texture, and also thickens the sauce.

1/4 pound extra-lean ground beef

1 small stalk celery, chopped (1/4 cup)

1 small onion, chopped (1/4 cup)

1 teaspoon Cajun seasonings blend

1 cup uncooked instant rice

1/4 cup chopped green pepper

1/2 cup water

4 medium fresh or 1/2 cup frozen (thawed) okra, sliced

1 medium tomato

1 can (11.5 ounces) light and tangy vegetable juice

Heat 10-inch nonstick skillet over medium-high heat. Cook ground beef, celery, onion and Cajun seasoning blend, stirring frequently, 4 minutes or until beef is brown and vegetables are tender. Stir in remaining ingredients. Reduce heat to medium-low. Cover and cook 5 minutes or until rice is tender.

1 Serving:		% Daily Value:	
Calories	500	Vitamin A	28%
Calories from fat	70	Vitamin C	40%
Fat, g	8	Calcium	10%
Saturated, g	3	Iron	32%
Cholesterol, mg	35		
Sodium, mg	640		
Carbohydrate, g	93		
Dietary Fiber, g	6		
Protein, g	21		

MEATY TIPS

The beef and pork available in markets today are leaner than ever. It still pays, though, to shop wisely. Look for cuts that are naturally lower in fat, such as loins, rounds and flank cuts, or that have the least visible fat in them. When purchasing ground beef, look for the extra-lean variety. And get in the habit of always trimming fat from meat before cooking. It's especially important not to overcook meat, since the leaner it is, the less tolerant it is to overcooking. Ground meats, steaks and chops are perhaps the easiest red meats to cook for two. Enjoy roasts when you have guests, since they are best when at least two pounds of meat is cooked. Or cook a roast, then freeze part of the leftovers.

Peppered Beef with Pasta

▯◖♡▮⩔

For a virtual rainbow of colors, use 1/4 cup each of three different colored bell peppers, rather than all green.

1/2 pound beef boneless sirloin steak, about 1/2 inch thick, cut into 2 pieces

1/2 teaspoon coarsely ground pepper

2 tablespoons tomato paste

1 tablespoon red wine vinegar

1 teaspoon fresh or 1/2 teaspoon dried thyme leaves

1 small onion, chopped (1/4 cup)

1 medium bell pepper, chopped (3/4 cup)

2 cups hot cooked bow tie pasta or soba noodles (2 ounces)

Rub both sides of beef pieces with coarsely ground pepper. Heat 10-inch nonstick skillet over medium-high heat. Cook beef 4 to 6 minutes on each side, turning once, until almost done. Add remaining ingredients except pasta. Reduce heat to medium-low. Cook, uncovered, 5 minutes or until beef is medium (160°). Serve sauce over beef and pasta.

1 Serving:		% Daily Value:	
Calories	330	Vitamin A	6%
Calories from fat	35	Vitamin C	34%
Fat, g	4	Calcium	4%
Saturated, g	1	Iron	26%
Cholesterol, mg	55		
Sodium, mg	170		
Carbohydrate, g	49		
Dietary Fiber, g	3		
Protein, g	28		

Veal with Mushrooms and Wine

▯◖

2 veal cutlets (about 4 ounces each)

2 teaspoons margarine or butter

1 clove garlic, finely chopped

Dash of salt

1/3 cup dry white wine or reduced-sodium chicken broth

1 tablespoon tomato paste

8 ounces mushrooms, sliced (about 3 cups)

1 tablespoon chopped fresh parsley

Trim fat from veal cutlets. Heat margarine and garlic in 10-inch skillet over medium heat until hot. Cook veal in margarine, turning once, 10 to 12 minutes for medium doneness (160°). Remove veal from skillet; sprinkle lightly with salt. Keep warm.

Mix wine and tomato paste in skillet. Stir in mushrooms. Cook, uncovered, 3 to 5 minutes, stirring occasionally, until mushrooms are tender. Serve mushroom mixture over veal. Sprinkle with parsley.

1 Serving:		% Daily Value:	
Calories	180	Vitamin A	8%
Calories from fat	70	Vitamin C	8%
Fat, g	8	Calcium	4%
Saturated, g	3	Iron	14%
Cholesterol, mg	75		
Sodium, mg	450		
Carbohydrate, g	8		
Dietary Fiber, g	1		
Protein, g	20		

Grilled Creole Pork and Peppers

4 banana peppers or 2 Anaheim chilies

2 tablespoons tomato paste

2 tablespoons water

2 teaspoons red wine vinegar

1/2 teaspoon reduced-sodium
   Worcestershire sauce

1/2 teaspoon Creole mustard*

1/2 teaspoon fresh or 1/8 teaspoon dried
   thyme leaves

1 butterflied pork chop or boneless loin
   chop, 3/4 inch thick (1/2 pound)

1 teaspoon ground Cajun seasoning blend
   for pork

Heat grill to low to moderate heat or set oven control to broil. Spray rack or broiler pan with nonstick cooking spray. Place peppers on grill or rack in broiler pan. Grill peppers 4 to 5 inches from heat about 4 minutes, turning several times, until skin is blistered and charred. Place peppers in paper bag. Close tightly; let stand 15 minutes.

Mix tomato paste, water, vinegar, Worcestershire sauce, mustard and thyme; set aside. Remove peppers from bag. Peel off skin; discard. Keep peppers warm.

Trim excess fat from pork chops. Slash outer edge of fat on pork 1/4 inch deep to prevent curling. Rub both sides of pork with Cajun seasoning blend. Place pork on rack or broiler pan. Grill pork 4 to 5 inches from heat 4 minutes or until seasoning browns; brush with tomato sauce. Grill 1 minute; turn. Grill 3 minutes longer; brush with sauce. Grill 1 to 2 minutes longer. Heat remaining sauce to boiling; serve over pork and peppers.

*1/2 teaspoon country-style Dijon mustard mixed with a dash of prepared horseradish may be substituted for the Creole mustard.

1 Serving:		% Daily Value:	
Calories	190	Vitamin A	50%
Calories from fat	70	Vitamin C	78%
Fat, g	8	Calcium	2%
Saturated, g	3	Iron	10%
Cholesterol, mg	65		
Sodium, mg	190		
Carbohydrate, g	8		
Dietary Fiber, g	1		
Protein, g	23		

Grilled Creole Pork and Peppers

Pork Chops with Kiwifruit-Mint Sauce

Kiwifruit-Mint Sauce (right)

**2 pork loin or rib chops, 3/4 inch thick
(about 2/3 pound)**

Dash of salt

Dash of pepper

Prepare Kiwifruit-Mint Sauce. Spray 10-inch nonstick skillet with nonstick cooking spray. Heat skillet over medium heat. Cook pork chops 9 to 10 minutes, turning once, until medium doneness (160°). Sprinkle with salt and pepper. Serve with Kiwifruit-Mint Sauce. Garnish with mint leaves if desired.

Kiwifruit-Mint Sauce

**1/2 kiwifruit, peeled and mashed
(2 tablespoons)**

**2 teaspoons chopped fresh or 1/4 teaspoon
dried mint leaves, crushed**

1 teaspoon sugar

1 teaspoon lime juice

Mix all ingredients.

1 Serving:		% Daily Value:	
Calories	185	Vitamin A	*
Calories from fat	70	Vitamin C	16%
Fat, g	8	Calcium	*
Saturated, g	3	Iron	4%
Cholesterol, mg	65		
Sodium, mg	310		
Carbohydrate, g	5		
Dietary Fiber, g	0		
Protein, g	23		

Ginger Pork in Orange Sauce

1 teaspoon ground ginger

1/2 teaspoon garlic powder

1/4 teaspoon pepper

1/2 pound lean boneless pork loin, cut into 1/2-inch cubes

3/4 cup orange juice

1 tablespoon packed brown sugar

1/2 teaspoon grated orange peel

4 ounces mushrooms, sliced (1 1/2 cups)

1 medium orange, peeled and sectioned

2 cups hot cooked couscous or rice

Mix ginger, garlic powder and pepper in plastic bag. Shake pork in seasonings. Heat 10-inch skillet over medium-high heat. Cook pork 2 to 3 minutes, stirring frequently to brown evenly. Stir in orange juice, brown sugar, orange peel and mushrooms. Reduce heat to low. Cover and cook about 15 minutes or until pork is tender. Stir in orange. Serve over couscous.

1 Serving:		% Daily Value:	
Calories	440	Vitamin A	2%
Calories from fat	65	Vitamin C	60%
Fat, g	7	Calcium	6%
Saturated, g	3	Iron	12%
Cholesterol, mg	50		
Sodium, mg	450		
Carbohydrate, g	70		
Dietary Fiber, g	4		
Protein, g	28		

Peppercorn Pork Tenderloin

Pork tenderloin is a tender, lower-fat and quick-to-fix meat. When you buy a whole tenderloin, cut it into 1/2-pound chunks to freeze for convenient two-person meals.

1 teaspoon olive oil

1/2 pound pork tenderloin, cut into 1/8-inch slices

1/2 teaspoon crushed green peppercorns

1/4 cup unsweetened apple juice

1 tablespoon lemon juice

1 tablespoon reduced-fat sour cream

2 cups hot cooked orzo

Chopped fresh parsley, if desired

Heat oil in 10-inch nonstick skillet over medium-high heat. Sprinkle both sides of pork with peppercorns. Sauté pork in oil 1 to 2 minutes on each side or until brown. Stir apple juice and lemon juice into skillet. Cook over low heat 2 minutes or until pork is brown. Stir in sour cream until blended. Serve pork and sauce over orzo. Sprinkle with parsley.

1 Serving:		% Daily Value:	
Calories	365	Vitamin A	2%
Calories from fat	65	Vitamin C	2%
Fat, g	7	Calcium	2%
Saturated, g	2	Iron	20%
Cholesterol, mg	70		
Sodium, mg	60		
Carbohydrate, g	45		
Dietary Fiber, g	1		
Protein, g	31		

Chicken and Noodles Paprikash

〤 ◗ ♥ ▯

1 teaspoon olive or vegetable oil

2 skinless boneless chicken breast halves (about 1/2 pound), cut into 1/2-inch strips

1/3 cup plain fat-free yogurt

2 teaspoons all-purpose flour

1/2 cup reduced-sodium chicken broth

1 teaspoon chopped fresh or 1/4 teaspoon dried thyme leaves

1 teaspoon paprika

1/2 medium onion, cut into thin wedges

2 cups hot cooked cholesterol-free noodles (about 4 ounces)

Heat oil in 10-inch nonstick skillet over medium-high heat until hot. Sauté chicken in oil 3 to 4 minutes or until no longer pink in center. Remove chicken from skillet; keep warm.

Mix yogurt and flour; reserve. Heat broth, thyme, paprika and onion to boiling in skillet; reduce heat. Simmer about 2 minutes, stirring occasionally, until onion is tender. Gradually stir yogurt mixture into broth mixture. Cook, stirring constantly, until thickened (do not boil). Stir chicken into sauce. Cook 1 minute longer. Serve chicken and sauce over noodles. Sprinkle with chopped green onion if desired.

1 Serving:		% Daily Value:	
Calories	350	Vitamin A	6%
Calories from fat	55	Vitamin C	2%
Fat, g	6	Calcium	10%
Saturated, g	1	Iron	18%
Cholesterol, mg	45		
Sodium, mg	180		
Carbohydrate, g	48		
Dietary Fiber, g	2		
Protein, g	28		

Chicken Fruit Salad

〤 ◖ ♥ ▯

1/3 cup plain fat-free yogurt

2 tablespoons fat-free mayonnaise or salad dressing

1 cup cubed cooked chicken breast

2/3 cup seedless green grapes

1 large peach, chopped (3/4 cup)

1 medium stalk celery, diced (1/2 cup)

1 teaspoon chopped fresh or 1/2 teaspoon dried mint leaves

Mix yogurt and mayonnaise in medium bowl until smooth. Stir in remaining ingredients. Cover and refrigerate at least 30 minutes or until chilled.

1 Serving:		% Daily Value:	
Calories	220	Vitamin A	4%
Calories from fat	25	Vitamin C	20%
Fat, g	3	Calcium	10%
Saturated, g	1	Iron	6%
Cholesterol, mg	55		
Sodium, mg	290		
Carbohydrate, g	25		
Dietary Fiber, g	2		
Protein, g	25		

Chicken Fruit Salad

Chicken Kabobs in Peanut Sauce

Photograph on page 46.

1/4 cup lime juice

2 tablespoons reduced-fat peanut butter

2 teaspoons grated lime peel

**1/2 teaspoon salt-free all-purpose spice and
   herb blend**

1/4 teaspoon ground ginger

**2 skinless boneless chicken breast halves
   (about 1/2 pound), cut into 1-inch
   pieces**

1 kiwifruit, peeled and chopped

**1 can (8 ounces) pineapple chunks in juice,
   drained and juice reserved**

2 cups hot cooked brown or wild rice

Place lime juice, peanut butter, lime peel, spice and herb blend and ginger in blender. Puree until blended. Place chicken in lime-peanut marinade. Cover and refrigerate at least 15 minutes but not more than 2 hours.

Set oven control to broil. Spray broiler pan with nonstick cooking spray. Drain chicken; reserve marinade. Thread chicken pieces on four 6-inch skewers, leaving space between each.* Place on rack in broiler pan. Broil chicken with tops 3 to 4 inches from heat 4 to 5 minutes. Turn and brush remaining marinade over chicken. Broil 3 to 4 minutes longer or until juice from chicken runs clear. Place kiwifruit and pineapple on bed of rice; top with skewers of chicken. Drizzle 1 tablespoon of the pineapple juice over chicken and rice.

*If using bamboo or wooden skewers, soak in water 30 minutes before using to prevent burning.

1 Serving:		% Daily Value:	
Calories	460	Vitamin A	*
Calories from fat	90	Vitamin C	44%
Fat, g	10	Calcium	6%
Saturated, g	3	Iron	12%
Cholesterol, mg	45		
Sodium, mg	140		
Carbohydrate, g	71		
Dietary Fiber, g	6		
Protein, g	27		

GOOD-FOR-YOU
CHICKEN FOR TWO

Boneless skinless chicken breasts are a good meat choice that is relatively low in fat and cholesterol. Here's an easy way to have it on hand, ready to cook. Several "batches" can be made up in minutes for the freezer. If frozen, place chicken in the refrigerator the night before you plan to use it, or in the morning before you leave for work.

Place two boneless skinless chicken breast halves (about 1/2 pound) and 1/4 cup fat-free marinade or salad dressing in 1-quart labeled, sealable, heavy-duty plastic freezer bag. (It's easier to label the bag before adding the chicken.) Turn to coat evenly. Press all air out of bag to reduce freezer burn; seal. Refrigerate 8 to 24 hours or freeze up to 2 months.

To prepare, cook thawed chicken according to one of the methods below:

On Top of the Stove

Heat 1 teaspoon oil in 10-inch nonstick skillet over medium heat. Add chicken. Cook 8 to 10 minutes, turning once, or until golden brown and juice of chicken is no longer pink when centers of thickest pieces are cut.

Broiling

Place chicken on rack in broiler pan. Broil 4 to 6 inches from heat 8 to 10 minutes, turning once, until juice is no longer pink when centers of thickest pieces are cut.

Grilling

Grill 4 to 6 inches from medium coals 10 to 15 minutes, turning once, until juice is no longer pink when centers of thickest pieces are cut.

Microwaving

Place on microwavable plate. Cover with waxed paper and microwave on high 3 to 5 minutes, rotating plate 1/2 turn after 2 minutes. Let stand 3 minutes.

Chicken and Avocado with Sweet Pepper Sauce

2 skinless boneless chicken breast halves
    (about 1/2 pound)

1/3 cup reduced-sodium chicken broth

1/2 teaspoon garlic powder

1/4 teaspoon pepper

1/2 red bell pepper, cut into chunks
    (3/4 cup)

1/4 cup apricot spreadable fruit, melted

1/4 ripe avocado, sliced

Place chicken breast halves, broth, garlic powder, pepper and bell pepper in 10-inch nonstick skillet. Heat to boiling; reduce heat. Cover and simmer about 10 minutes or until juice of chicken is no longer pink when centers of thickest pieces are cut. Remove chicken; keep warm. Pour broth mixture into blender; add spreadable fruit. Blend until red peppers are pureed. Slice chicken breasts crosswise. Arrange avocado and chicken slices on plates; top with red pepper sauce.

1 Serving:		% Daily Value:	
Calories	220	Vitamin A	12%
Calories from fat	55	Vitamin C	32%
Fat, g	6	Calcium	2%
Saturated, g	1	Iron	8%
Cholesterol, mg	45		
Sodium, mg	115		
Carbohydrate, g	27		
Dietary Fiber, g	5		
Protein, g	19		

Easy Chicken-Pasta Primavera

For about half the calories and fat of the traditional recipe, you can enjoy meat, vegetables and pasta all in one tasty dish!

4 ounces uncooked fettuccine

1 cup broccoli flowerets

1/2 cup 1/4-inch strips carrot

1 teaspoon olive or vegetable oil

2 skinless boneless chicken breast halves
    (about 1/2 pound), cut into 1/2-inch
    strips

1 clove garlic, finely chopped

1/3 cup fat-free ranch dressing

2 tablespoons grated reduced-fat Parmesan
    cheese blend

1 teaspoon shredded fresh or 1/8 teaspoon
    dried basil leaves

Cook and drain fettuccine as directed on package—except add broccoli and carrot 1 minute before pasta is done. While pasta is cooking, heat oil in 10-inch nonstick skillet over medium-high heat until hot. Sauté chicken and garlic in oil 2 to 3 minutes until chicken is no longer pink in center; remove from heat. Stir in dressing, cheese and basil. Toss with pasta and vegetables.

1 Serving:		% Daily Value:	
Calories	405	Vitamin A	62%
Calories from fat	110	Vitamin C	36%
Fat, g	12	Calcium	14%
Saturated, g	2	Iron	20%
Cholesterol, mg	100		
Sodium, mg	560		
Carbohydrate, g	50		
Dietary Fiber, g	5		
Protein, g	29		

Easy Chicken-Pasta Primavera

Chicken Salad Pita Sandwiches

�� ◊ ♡ ♦

1 cup chopped cooked chicken breast

1/4 cup fat-free honey Dijon dressing

1/4 cup chopped cucumber

1/4 cup chopped tomato

1 tablespoon finely chopped cashews

2 whole wheat pita breads (6 inches in diameter), cut into halves to form pockets

2 tablespoons fat-free mayonnaise or salad dressing

1/2 cup alfalfa sprouts

Mix chicken, dressing, cucumber, tomato and cashews. Cover and refrigerate at least 30 minutes or until chilled. Just before serving, spread insides of pita pockets with mayonnaise. Fill pockets with chicken mixture; top with alfalfa sprouts.

1 Sandwich:		% Daily Value:	
Calories	315	Vitamin A	2%
Calories from fat	90	Vitamin C	10%
Fat, g	10	Calcium	4%
Saturated, g	3	Iron	12%
Cholesterol, mg	55		
Sodium, mg	640		
Carbohydrate, g	32		
Dietary Fiber, g	4		
Protein, g	28		

Curried Chicken Pomegranate

X ◊ ♡ ▮

Pomegranates are in season in the United States only in October and November, but they can be stored in the refrigerator up to two months. Half a medium pomegranate should yield about 1/2 cup seeds.

1/2 cup plain fat-free yogurt

1/2 to 1 teaspoon curry powder

1/4 teaspoon ground ginger

1/2 cup pomegranate seeds*

1 large clove garlic, finely chopped

2 skinless boneless chicken breast halves (about 1/2 pound)

1 1/2 teaspoons chopped fresh or 1/2 teaspoon dried mint leaves

Heat oven to 350°. Spray square baking dish, 8×8×2 inches, with nonstick cooking spray. Mix yogurt, curry powder, ginger, pomegranate seeds and garlic in medium bowl. Dip chicken in yogurt mixture; place in baking dish. Spread remaining yogurt mixture over chicken. Bake 35 to 45 minutes or until juices run clear. Sprinkle with mint.

*One large roma (plum) tomato, chopped (1/2 cup), can be substituted for the pomegranate seeds.

1 Serving:		% Daily Value:	
Calories	155	Vitamin A	*
Calories from fat	25	Vitamin C	2%
Fat, g	3	Calcium	14%
Saturated, g	1	Iron	6%
Cholesterol, mg	45		
Sodium, mg	90		
Carbohydrate, g	12		
Dietary Fiber, g	1		
Protein, g	21		

Curried Chicken Pomegranate

Vegetable-Turkey Loaf

1/2 pound ground turkey

1 slice bread, torn into small pieces

1/4 cup fat-free egg product or 2 egg whites

1/4 cup shredded carrot

2 tablespoons chopped onion

2 tablespoons green bell pepper

2 tablespoons chopped celery

2 tablespoons chili sauce or ketchup

1/8 teaspoon salt

Dash of pepper

Dash of garlic powder

2 tablespoons chili sauce or ketchup

Heat oven to 350°. Mix all ingredients except the last 2 tablespoons chili sauce. Shape mixture into loaf in center of ungreased shallow baking pan. Spoon 2 tablespoons chili sauce over loaf. Bake uncovered about 45 minutes or until no longer pink in center.

1 Serving:		% Daily Value:	
Calories	290	Vitamin A	26%
Calories from fat	110	Vitamin C	10%
Fat, g	12	Calcium	4%
Saturated, g	4	Iron	12%
Cholesterol, mg	75		
Sodium, mg	700		
Carbohydrate, g	18		
Dietary Fiber, g	1		
Protein, g	28		

Santa Fe Turkey Salad

1 cup cut-up cooked turkey

2 tablespoons fat-free sour cream

2 tablespoons fat-free mayonnaise or salad dressing

2 tablespoons chopped onion

2 tablespoons finely chopped carrot

1 tablespoon chopped fresh cilantro

1 tablespoon lime juice

1 tablespoon capers

1 tablespoon diced pimientos

1/4 teaspoon ground cumin

1 teaspoon chopped fresh or 1/4 teaspoon dried oregano leaves

Lettuce leaves

1/4 avocado, cut into wedges

Toss all ingredients except lettuce and avocado. Serve salad on lettuce. Garnish with avocado. Sprinkle with paprika if desired.

1 Serving:		% Daily Value:	
Calories	195	Vitamin A	20%
Calories from fat	70	Vitamin C	22%
Fat, g	8	Calcium	6%
Saturated, g	2	Iron	12%
Cholesterol, mg	60		
Sodium, mg	270		
Carbohydrate, g	10		
Dietary Fiber, g	2		
Protein, g	23		

Catfish with Mustard Sauce

This recipe enhances the naturally sweet flavor of catfish—even people who usually don't like fish will like this preparation. Try serving it with saffron rice, crisp carrot sticks and corn muffins.

1/2 pound catfish fillets

1/2 teaspoon ground Cajun seasonings

2 tablespoons country-Dijon mustard

4 black olives, chopped

Move oven rack to position slightly above middle of oven. Heat oven to 450°. Spray square baking dish, 8×8×2 inches, with nonstick coating spray. Coat both sides of fillets with Cajun seasonings and mustard. Place in baking dish. Sprinkle with olives. Bake 12 to 14 minutes or until fish flakes easily with fork.

1 Serving:		% Daily Value:	
Calories	125	Vitamin A	2%
Calories from fat	25	Vitamin C	*
Fat, g	3	Calcium	4%
Saturated, g	1	Iron	4%
Cholesterol, mg	60		
Sodium, mg	350		
Carbohydrate, g	2		
Dietary Fiber, g	0		
Protein, g	22		

NOTHING FISHY ABOUT FAT

Fish comes in many varities and in several forms. Fresh fish is increasingly available as it grows in popularity as a healthy food choice and, for two, is easiest to purchase in fillets and steaks. Frozen fish is available individually quick frozen so just one or two pieces (depending on the size) can be used at a time. Most fish is less fatty than lean ground meat, which is about 15 percent fat. Fish classified as lean has less than 2 1/2 percent fat; medium-fat fish has 2 1/5 to 5 percent fat; and fatty fish has greater than 5 percent fat.

Lean	Medium-Fat	Fatty
Bass, sea	Anchovy	Butterfish
Bass, striped	Bluefish	Carp
Cod	Catfish	Eel
Flounder	Croaker	Herring
Grouper	Mullet	Mackerel, Atlantic
Haddock	Porgy	Mackerel, Pacific
Halibut	Redfish	Mackerel, Spanish
Mackerel, king	Salmon, pink	Pompano
Mahimahi	Shark	Sablefish
Orange roughy	Swordfish	Salmon, Chinook
Perch, ocean	Trout, rainbow	Salmon, sockeye
Pike, northern	Trout, sea	Sardines
Pike, walleye	Tuna, bluefin	Shad
Pollock	Turbot	Trout, lake
Red snapper	Whitefish	Tuna, albacore
Scrod		
Sole		
Tuna, skipjack		
Tuna, yellowfin		
Whiting		

Baked Honey Walleye

1/2 pound walleye or other firm white-flesh fish fillet

1/4 cup fresh parsley sprigs, lightly packed

1 teaspoon fresh or 1/2 teaspoon dried thyme leaves

1/4 teaspoon garlic powder

10 buttery reduced-fat snack crackers

1 tablespoon honey

1 tablespoon lemon juice

Lemon wedges

Move oven rack to position slightly above middle of oven. Heat oven to 500°. Spray pie plate, 9×1 1/2 inches, with nonstick cooking spray. Cut fillet into 2×2-inch pieces. Place parsley, thyme, garlic powder and crackers in blender or food processor. Cover and pulse until mixture forms fine crumbs. Place crumb mixture in plastic bag. Beat honey and lemon in medium bowl; stir in fish pieces. Place a few fish pieces at a time in bag; shake to coat with crumb mixture. Repeat with remaining fish.

Place fish in pie plate. Bake, uncovered, about 10 to 12 minutes or until fish flakes easily with fork. Serve with lemon wedges.

1 Serving:		% Daily Value:	
Calories	190	Vitamin A	4%
Calories from fat	35	Vitamin C	10%
Fat, g	4	Calcium	4%
Saturated, g	0	Iron	12%
Cholesterol, mg	50		
Sodium, mg	220		
Carbohydrate, g	19		
Dietary Fiber, g	1		
Protein, g	21		

Smothered Orange Roughy

Half the fun of cooking food in a pouch is opening it at the table! Take the packets to the table and open for a tasty treat.

1/2 cup lemon juice

1 teaspoon walnut, avocado or vegetable oil

1/2 pound orange roughy fillets

1 1/2 teaspoons chopped fresh or 1/2 teaspoon dried marjoram leaves

1/8 teaspoon salt

2 medium roma (plum) tomatoes, chopped (3/4 cup)

1/2 bell pepper, cut into rings

1 small onion, sliced (3/4 cup)

Mix lemon juice and walnut oil. Pour over fillets. Cover and refrigerate at least 15 minutes but not more than 1 hour. Drain fish; discard marinade.

Heat oven to 375°. Sprinkle fish with marjoram and salt. Place fish fillets on 12- to 15-inch piece of aluminum foil or parchment paper. Top with tomatoes, bell pepper and onion. Wrap fish in foil, sealing tightly. Place on cookie sheet. Bake 15 minutes or until fish flakes easily with fork.

1 Serving:		% Daily Value:	
Calories	130	Vitamin A	8%
Calories from fat	20	Vitamin C	32%
Fat, g	2	Calcium	2%
Saturated, g	1	Iron	4%
Cholesterol, mg	55		
Sodium, mg	240		
Carbohydrate, g	9		
Dietary Fiber, g	2		
Protein, g	21		

Smothered Orange Roughy

Hawaiian Broiled Cod with Rice

1 can (8 ounces) pineapple in juice, drained and juice reserved

2 tablespoons orange juice

1 teaspoon grated orange peel

2 teaspoons soy sauce

1/2 pound cod or other firm white fish fillet

2 cups hot cooked rice

1/2 orange, peeled and chopped

1 green onion, chopped

1 tablespoon coconut, toasted, if desired

Set oven control to broil. Spray broiler pan with nonstick cooking spray. Mix 1/3 cup of the reserved pineapple juice, the orange juice, orange peel and soy sauce. Cut fillet into 2 pieces. Marinate fish in sauce 5 minutes; remove. Place on rack in broiler pan. Broil fish with tops 4 to 5 inches from heat 6 to 8 minutes or until fish flakes easily with fork.

Meanwhile, heat marinade to boiling in 1-quart saucepan; reduce heat to low. Simmer 3 minutes, stirring occasionally. Toss marinade with pineapple, rice, orange and green onion. Serve fish over fruited rice. Top with toasted coconut if desired.

1 Serving:		% Daily Value:	
Calories	380	Vitamin A	2%
Calories from fat	20	Vitamin C	28%
Fat, g	2	Calcium	6%
Saturated, g	1	Iron	14%
Cholesterol, mg	55		
Sodium, mg	430		
Carbohydrate, g	69		
Dietary Fiber, g	3		
Protein, g	24		

Italian Flounder

1/2 pound flounder or other lean fish fillet

Dash of salt

1 teaspoon chopped fresh or 1/4 teaspoon dried oregano leaves

Dash of paprika

2 tomato slices (1/2 inch thick)

1 teaspoon chopped fresh chives

2 tablespoons fat-free Italian dressing

2 teaspoons grated reduced-fat Parmesan cheese blend

Heat oven to 450°. Spray square baking dish, 8×8×2 inches, with nonstick cooking spray. Cut fillet into 2 pieces. Place in baking dish. Sprinkle with salt, oregano and paprika. Place tomato on fish; sprinkle with chives. Pour dressing over chives; sprinkle with cheese. Bake, uncovered, 12 to 15 minutes or until fish flakes easily with fork.

1 Serving:		% Daily Value:	
Calories	95	Vitamin A	4%
Calories from fat	10	Vitamin C	4%
Fat, g	1	Calcium	4%
Saturated, g	0	Iron	4%
Cholesterol, mg	50		
Sodium, mg	370		
Carbohydrate, g	3		
Dietary Fiber, g	1		
Protein, g	19		

Salmon with Creamy Parsley Sauce

Creamy Parsley Sauce (right)

1 cup water

1/2 cup dry white wine or water

1/8 teaspoon salt

1/8 teaspoon pepper

1 teaspoon chopped fresh or 1/4 teaspoon
dried thyme leaves

1 teaspoon chopped fresh or 1/4 teaspoon
dried tarragon leaves

2 small salmon steaks, each 1 inch thick
(3/4 pound)

2 lemon slices, each 1/8 inch thick

Prepare Creamy Parsley Sauce. Heat water, wine, salt, pepper, thyme and tarragon to boiling in 10-inch skillet; reduce heat. Cover and simmer 5 minutes. Place fish steaks in skillet. Add water, if necessary, to cover. Heat to boiling; reduce heat. Simmer, uncovered, 12 to 15 minutes or until fish flakes easily with fork.

Carefully remove fish with slotted spatula; drain on wire rack. Carefully remove skin if desired. Serve with Creamy Parsley Sauce; garnish with lemon slices.

Creamy Parsley Sauce

1/2 cup fresh parsley sprigs, lightly packed

3/4 cup fat-free cottage cheese

1 1/2 teaspoons lemon juice

1 1/2 teaspoons low-fat milk

1 teaspoon chopped fresh or 1/4 teaspoon
dried basil leaves

1/4 teaspoon salt

Dash of pepper

2 to 3 drops red pepper sauce

Place all ingredients in blender. Cover and blend on high speed about 3 minutes, stopping blender occasionally to scrape sides, until smooth.

1 Serving:		% Daily Value:	
Calories	270	Vitamin A	16%
Calories from fat	80	Vitamin C	20%
Fat, g	9	Calcium	14%
Saturated, g	3	Iron	10%
Cholesterol, mg	95		
Sodium, mg	650		
Carbohydrate, g	6		
Dietary Fiber, g	1		
Protein, g	42		

3

Meatless Dishes

Cheese Enchiladas (page 86), Southwestern Corn Salad (page 118)

Cheese and Noodle Bake

1 cup uncooked cholesterol-free noodles (2 ounces)

1/2 cup fat-free cottage cheese

1/3 cup shredded fat-free Cheddar cheese

1/4 cup fat-free sour cream

1 green onion, chopped

1 tablespoon grated reduced-fat Parmesan cheese blend

1/4 teaspoon reduced-sodium Worcestershire sauce

Dash of pepper

1/2 cup fat-free egg product or 3 egg whites

Heat oven to 350°. Spray 9-inch pie plate with nonstick cooking spray. Cook noodles as directed on package; drain. Mix remaining ingredients into noodles. Spread in pie plate. Bake uncovered about 25 minutes or until center is set and edges are golden brown. Let stand 5 minutes before serving.

1 Serving:		% Daily Value:	
Calories	370	Vitamin A	18%
Calories from fat	35	Vitamin C	*
Fat, g	4	Calcium	30%
Saturated, g	2	Iron	18%
Cholesterol, mg	110		
Sodium, mg	600		
Carbohydrate, g	60		
Dietary Fiber, g	2		
Protein, g	28		

Couscous and Lentil Pilaf

2 cups hot cooked couscous

1 cup cooked lentils

1 small tomato, chopped (about 1/2 cup)

2 tablespoons raisins

1 tablespoon chopped fresh or 1 teaspoon dried mint leaves

Dash of freshly ground pepper

Dash of ground red pepper (cayenne)

1/4 cup plain fat-free yogurt

Heat oven to 400°. Grease 1 1/2-quart casserole. Mix all ingredients; spoon into casserole. Cover and bake about 20 minutes or until hot. Serve with yogurt.

1 Serving:		% Daily Value:	
Calories	345	Vitamin A	4%
Calories from fat	10	Vitamin C	8%
Fat, g	1	Calcium	10%
Saturated, g	0	Iron	24%
Cholesterol, mg	0		
Sodium, mg	440		
Carbohydrate, g	74		
Dietary Fiber, g	8		
Protein, g	18		

Szechuan Eggplant Linguine

Use any thin-strand pasta, such as angel hair, Chinese or even soba (buckwheat) noodles for this truly international dish. Szechuan is synonymous with fiery hot taste—taste the sauce and pick the heat level that's right for you. If Japanese eggplant is not available, a small eggplant can be used.

1 teaspoon vegetable oil

1 medium Japanese eggplant, chopped
(about 1 1/2 cups)

3/4 cup reduced-sodium chunky garlic and
onion spaghetti sauce

1 to 2 teaspoons Szechuan hot and spicy
sauce*

2 cups hot cooked cholesterol-free linguine
(4 ounces)

1/2 teaspoon freshly grated gingerroot,
if desired

Heat oil in 1-quart saucepan over medium-high heat. Sauté eggplant in oil. Stir in spaghetti and Szechuan sauces; reduce heat to medium. Cook 2 minutes, stirring occasionally, until hot. Pour sauce over hot linguine. Sprinkle with gingerroot.

*Chinese chile sauce or Italian chile pepper sauce may be substituted for the Szechuan hot and spicy sauce.

1 Serving:		% Daily Value:	
Calories	305	Vitamin A	14%
Calories from fat	65	Vitamin C	16%
Fat, g	4	Calcium	6%
Saturated, g	1	Iron	18%
Cholesterol, mg	0		
Sodium, mg	60		
Carbohydrate, g	62		
Dietary Fiber, g	6		
Protein, g	9		

Dijon Tomato Pasta

2 cups uncooked bow tie pasta (4 ounces)

6 sun-dried tomato halves (not oil-packed)

1 teaspoon olive or vegetable oil

1 medium onion, thinly sliced
(about 1/2 cup)

2 cloves garlic, finely chopped

1 cup reduced-sodium chicken or vegetable
broth

2 tablespoons tomato paste

1 tablespoon chopped fresh or 1 teaspoon
dried basil leaves

2 teaspoons Dijon mustard

2 teaspoons grated reduced-fat Italian cheese
blend

Cook and drain pasta as directed on package—except do not add salt. Meanwhile, cover tomato halves with boiling water; let stand 5 minutes. Drain and chop. Heat oil in 10-inch nonstick skillet over medium-high heat. Sauté onion and garlic in oil; reduce heat to medium. Stir in tomato halves, broth, tomato paste, basil and mustard. Cook 3 minutes, stirring occasionally, until sauce has thickened slightly. Stir in pasta. Sprinkle with cheese.

1 Serving:		% Daily Value:	
Calories	295	Vitamin A	6%
Calories from fat	45	Vitamin C	10%
Fat, g	5	Calcium	6%
Saturated, g	1	Iron	18%
Cholesterol, mg	0		
Sodium, mg	550		
Carbohydrate, g	55		
Dietary Fiber, g	4		
Protein, g	11		

Olive Paprika Penne

1 1/2 cups uncooked penne or macaroni pasta (4 ounces)

1 teaspoon olive oil

1 cup thinly sliced mushrooms (3 ounces)

1 medium onion, chopped (about 1/2 cup)

1 cup Italian seasoned chunky tomato sauce

1 teaspoon paprika

12 pimiento-stuffed olives

2 to 4 teaspoons grated reduced-fat Parmesan cheese blend

Basil leaves, if desired

Cook and drain pasta as directed on package—except do not add salt. Meanwhile, heat oil in 2-quart saucepan over medium-high heat. Sauté mushrooms and onion in oil; reduce heat to medium. Stir in pasta, tomato sauce, paprika and olives. Cook, stirring occasionally, until hot. Sprinkle with cheese. Garnish with basil if desired.

1 Serving:		% Daily Value:	
Calories	325	Vitamin A	16%
Calories from fat	65	Vitamin C	26%
Fat, g	7	Calcium	10%
Saturated, g	1	Iron	24%
Cholesterol, mg	0		
Sodium, mg	1,030		
Carbohydrate, g	59		
Dietary Fiber, g	5		
Protein, g	11		

Black Bean–Pasta Cancun

2 cups uncooked radiatore (nugget) pasta (4 ounces)

1 can (14.5 ounces) diced tomatoes with chili spices

1 cup black beans, rinsed and drained

1/2 teaspoon grated lime peel

1/4 teaspoon ground cumin

1/4 bell pepper, cut into 2×1/4-inch strips

2 tablespoons fat-free sour cream

2 lime wedges

Cilantro leaves, if desired

Cook and drain pasta as directed on package—except do not add salt. Meanwhile, heat tomatoes to boiling in 2-quart saucepan. Stir in pasta, beans, lime peel, cumin and bell pepper; reduce heat to low. Cover and cook 2 to 3 minutes, stirring occasionally, until hot. Garnish with sour cream, lime and cilantro. Squeeze lime over pasta.

1 Serving:		% Daily Value:	
Calories	335	Vitamin A	16%
Calories from fat	25	Vitamin C	40%
Fat, g	3	Calcium	14%
Saturated, g	0	Iron	30%
Cholesterol, mg	5		
Sodium, mg	570		
Carbohydrate, g	71		
Dietary Fiber, g	10		
Protein, g	16		

Black Bean–Pasta Cancun

White Bean Stew

4 SERVINGS

This tasty stew is packed with fiber, and freezes very well. It also keeps nicely in the refrigerator for up to one week.

1/4 cup dried lentils

1 tablespoon olive oil

1 medium onion, chopped (about 1/2 cup)

1 medium stalk celery, chopped (about 1/2 cup)

1/4 cup diced green bell pepper

1 clove garlic, finely chopped

1 tablespoon parsley flakes

1/8 teaspoon pepper

1 can (15 ounces) cannellini beans, rinsed and drained

1 can (14 1/2 ounces) reduced-sodium chicken or vegetable broth

1 can (14 ounces) chunky Italian-style tomatoes and seasonings, undrained

Pour 1 cup boiling water over lentils in a small bowl. Let stand at least 15 minutes; drain. Heat oil in 3-quart saucepan over medium-high heat. Sauté onion, celery, bell pepper and garlic in oil. Stir in parsley and pepper. Add lentils, beans, broth and tomatoes. Heat to boiling; reduce heat. Cover and simmer 30 minutes or until vegetables are tender.

1 Serving:		% Daily Value:	
Calories	235	Vitamin A	6%
Calories from fat	45	Vitamin C	20%
Fat, g	5	Calcium	14%
Saturated, g	1	Iron	34%
Cholesterol, mg	0		
Sodium, mg	730		
Carbohydrate, g	40		
Dietary Fiber, g	9		
Protein, g	16		

Red Beans and Rice

1 teaspoon vegetable oil

1 small onion, chopped (1/4 cup)

1 small green bell pepper, chopped (1/2 cup)

1 clove garlic, crushed

1 teaspoon chopped fresh or 1/4 teaspoon dried thyme leaves

1/4 teaspoon salt

1/2 teaspoon red pepper sauce

1 can (15 to 16 ounces) reduced-sodium kidney beans, rinsed and drained

1/2 package (10 ounces) frozen cut okra, thawed

2 cups hot cooked rice

1 small tomato, seeded and chopped (1/2 cup)

Heat oil in 10-inch skillet over medium-high heat. Cook onion, bell pepper and garlic in oil about 2 minutes, stirring occasionally. Stir in remaining ingredients except rice and tomato. Cook, stirring occasionally, until mixture is hot. Serve with rice. Top with tomato.

1 Serving:		% Daily Value:	
Calories	395	Vitamin A	6%
Calories from fat	35	Vitamin C	30%
Fat, g	4	Calcium	12%
Saturated, g	1	Iron	38%
Cholesterol, mg	0		
Sodium, mg	960		
Carbohydrate, g	87		
Dietary Fiber, g	15		
Protein, g	18		

Red Beans and Rice

Spinach-Barley Risotto

Pearl barley gives this dish the creaminess of the traditional long-cooking risotto that uses arborio rice, and it cuts cooking time! You can also use quick-cooking barley—it reduces cooking time even more as there is no presoaking, but the dish won't be quite as creamy.

2 teaspoons olive oil

1 cup thinly sliced mushrooms (4 ounces)

1 medium onion, chopped (1/2 cup)

1 1/2 cups reduced-sodium chicken or
    vegetable broth

1 teaspoon garlic pepper seasoning blend

1 teaspoon Dijon mustard

3/4 cup uncooked quick-cooking barley or
    pearl barley, presoaked*

1/3 cup instant wild rice

1/4 cup dried cranberries

2 cups packed spinach leaves, shredded
    (3 ounces)

Heat oil in 10-inch nonstick skillet over high heat. Cook mushrooms and onion in oil. Stir in broth, garlic pepper seasoning blend and mustard. Cover and heat to boiling. Stir in remaining ingredients, except spinach; reduce heat to low. Cover and simmer 10 minutes, stirring once. Stir in spinach; cover and simmer about 5 minutes or until water is absorbed and barley and wild rice are tender.

*Presoak pearl barley in 2 cups of water at least 5 hours or overnight; drain.

1 Serving:		% Daily Value:	
Calories	450	Vitamin A	46%
Calories from fat	65	Vitamin C	20%
Fat, g	7	Calcium	10%
Saturated, g	1	Iron	26%
Cholesterol, mg	0		
Sodium, mg	580		
Carbohydrate, g	95		
Dietary Fiber, g	14		
Protein, g	16		

No Beans About It

Dried beans, peas and lentils are part of the legumes food category. They are cholesterol-free, low in fat and sodium (unless canned) and an excellent source of complex carbohydrates, fiber and calcium.

- When cooking for two, it can be more efficient to use canned or frozen beans rather than cooking beans from the dried state. Always rinse and drain them, unless the recipe calls for undrained, to eliminate some of the sodium.

- A variety of beans are available canned: kidney (light or dark), pinto, northern, black, butter and lima are just a few.

- Lentils cook in a much shorter amount of time (about 20 minutes) and are more suitable for smaller cooking amounts.

- Make main dishes containing beans like chili and freeze in smaller serving portions. Most beans freeze quite well, although occasionally the skin of some may break.

Spinach-Barley Risotto

Stuffed Hot Chilies

⟨symbols⟩

Take advantage of the abundance of fresh peppers when they are in season and at their most inexpensive. This versatile stuffing will fill two larger roasted peppers such as bell or poblano peppers. You can vary the heat of the dish by adjusting the amount of hot jalapeño pepper and the cooling yogurt topping.

2 tablespoons uncooked bulgur

1/3 cup frozen (thawed) corn with red peppers

1/3 cup grated fat-free mozzarella cheese

1/2 teaspoon chopped fresh jalapeño pepper

1 teaspoon chopped fresh or 1/4 teaspoon marjoram leaves

1/4 teaspoon garlic powder

2 cans (4 ounces each) roasted whole chile peppers or 4 fresh Anaheim chilies, roasted and peeled

1/4 cup low-sodium salsa

1/4 cup plain fat-free yogurt

Heat oven to 350°. Spray square baking dish, 8×8×2 inches, with nonstick cooking spray. Pour 1/3 cup boiling water over bulgur in medium bowl. Let stand, stirring occasionally, 10 minutes or until water is absorbed. Stir in corn, 1/4 cup of the cheese, the jalapeño pepper, marjoram and garlic powder. Slice chilies along one side; remove ribs and seeds. Drain well.

Stuff about 1/4 cup filling into each chile. Place seam side down in baking dish. Top with salsa and remaining cheese. Bake, uncovered, 25 to 30 minutes or until hot. Just before serving, spoon yogurt over chilies.

1 Serving:		% Daily Value:	
Calories	155	Vitamin A	26%
Calories from fat	10	Vitamin C	60%
Fat, g	1	Calcium	22%
Saturated, g	2	Iron	6%
Cholesterol, mg	0		
Sodium, mg	1,200		
Carbohydrate, g	23		
Dietary Fiber, g	4		
Protein, g	10		

CARBO LOADING WITH PERFECT PASTA

Pasta is available dried, fresh and in some parts of the country, frozen. Dried pasta is the most common and many shapes and sizes are available in boxes or packages and in bulk form. Pasta is an excellent source of complex carbohydrate.

- For each serving, use 2 ounces dried or 3 ounces refrigerated pasta. Fresh pasta takes about 1/4 of the cooking time of dried pasta. Cooking times will vary according to the shape.

- To measure 4 ounces of spaghetti easily, make a circle with your thumb and index finger, about the size of a quarter, and fill it with pasta.

- Use a 3-quart saucepan when cooking pasta for two. During cooking, the pasta should move freely in the boiling water.

- Begin with cold water and salt the water only if desired. Bring the water to a rolling boil (bubbles break the surface of the water) before adding the pasta. Covering the pan while heating over high heat will shorten the time it takes to bring the water to a boil.

- Add olive or vegetable oil to the water only if you plan to make a cold pasta salad, as it makes pasta slippery. Hot sauces cling much better to pasta cooked in water with no oil added. The addition of oil (1/4 teaspoon) will also reduce foaming.

- Cook the pasta uncovered. The heat can be reduced, but keep the water boiling so the pasta does not stick together. Stir occasionally to prevent sticking on the bottom of the pan.

- Make pasta easier to use and serve by cooking a quantity, then wrapping and refrigerating or freezing the extra amounts in small freezer bags for use at a later time. To reheat, immerse plain pasta in boiling water until hot, about 1 minute. Or, microwave, covered, about 1 minute per cup.

Brown Rice–Nut Loaf

3 SERVINGS (2 SLICES EACH)

Would you like your meal to have a Southwest flavor? Try substituting 1/2 cup refried beans for the cream cheese and then top with salsa and cilantro.

1 teaspoon vegetable oil

1 medium onion, chopped (1/2 cup)

1 medium carrot, shredded (1/2 cup)

1 small green bell pepper, chopped (1/2 cup)

3 tablespoons chopped roasted unsalted cashews

1/2 teaspoon garlic powder

1/4 teaspoon salt

1/8 teaspoon pepper

1 cup cooked brown rice

1/4 cup fat-free soft cream cheese

2 tablespoons fat-free egg product or 1 egg white

Heat oven to 350°. Heat oil in 10-inch nonstick skillet over medium-high heat. Sauté onion, carrot and bell pepper in oil. Stir in 2 tablespoons cashews, the garlic powder, salt and pepper; mix until blended. Remove from heat. Mix in rice, cream cheese and egg product until blended. Pack into nonstick small loaf pan, 6×3×2 1/2 inches. Sprinkle with 1 tablespoon cashews.

Bake 30 to 35 minutes or until firm and slightly browned. Cool 10 minutes. Remove from pan; slice.

2 Slices:		% Daily Value:	
Calories	170	Vitamin A	32%
Calories from fat	55	Vitamin C	14%
Fat, g	6	Calcium	4%
Saturated, g	1	Iron	4%
Cholesterol, mg	0		
Sodium, mg	330		
Carbohydrate, g	24		
Dietary Fiber, g	3		
Protein, g	8		

<table>
<tr><td>

COMPLEMENTING COMBINATIONS

Learning how to complete meatless protein sources is important for vegetarians and for people in cultures where animal foods are not eaten. However, for most of us who eat a varied daily diet, protein completion is somewhat less important. Mix and match foods from the first column with those in the second to achieve complete proteins.

Legumes	*Grains, Nuts & Seeds*
kidney	*corn bread*
lentils	*white or brown rice*
navy	*pasta*
garbanzo (chick peas)	*rye bread*
pinto	*cashews and sunflower*
black	*nuts*
tofu (bean curd)	*corn or flour tortillas*
lima	*tahini (sesame-seed paste)*
peanuts or peanut butter	*whole-grain rolls*
	couscous
peas or split peas	*whole wheat pita bread*
soybeans	*barley*
black-eyed peas	*almonds and pumpkin*
cranberry	*seeds*
adzuki	*bulgur*
mung	*walnuts and sesame seeds*
great northern	*wheat germ*
	oat bran muffin

</td></tr>
</table>

Barley-Bean Stew

1 teaspoon vegetable oil

1 medium onion, chopped (1/2 cup)

1/4 cup chopped celery

2 1/2 cups tomato juice

1/4 cup uncooked quick-cooking barley

1 to 1 1/2 teaspoons chili powder

1/4 teaspoon salt

1/8 teaspoon pepper

1 can (15- to 16-ounce size) great northern or navy beans, rinsed and drained

2 tablespoons chopped fresh parsley

Heat oil in 10-inch skillet over medium-high heat. Cook onion and celery in oil about 2 minutes, stirring occasionally. Stir in remaining ingredients except parsley; heat to boiling. Reduce heat; cover and simmer about 20 minutes until barley is tender and stew is desired consistency. Stir in parsley.

1 Serving:		**% Daily Value:**	
Calories	415	Vitamin A	24%
Calories from fat	35	Vitamin C	54%
Fat, g	4	Calcium	24%
Saturated, g	1	Iron	58%
Cholesterol, mg	0		
Sodium, mg	1,600		
Carbohydrate, g	88		
Dietary Fiber, g	18		
Protein, g	25		

Curry Beans and Rice

Think you don't like beans? We predict that the tantalizing aroma of curry and honey will change your mind!

1 cup instant brown rice

1/2 cup chopped fresh or frozen broccoli

1 teaspoon vegetable oil

3 green onions, sliced

1 to 2 teaspoons curry powder

2 tablespoons honey

1 can (16 ounces) baked beans, undrained

1 tablespoon chopped toasted slivered almonds

Cook rice according to package directions—except omit salt and add broccoli. Heat oil in 2-quart saucepan over high heat. Cook onions and curry powder in oil. Stir in rice mixture, honey and beans. Cover and cook 2 to 3 minutes or until hot. Sprinkle each serving with almonds.

1 Serving:		% Daily Value:	
Calories	640	Vitamin A	4%
Calories from fat	80	Vitamin C	22%
Fat, g	9	Calcium	18%
Saturated, g	1	Iron	34%
Cholesterol, mg	0		
Sodium, mg	930		
Carbohydrate, g	134		
Dietary Fiber, g	18		
Protein, g	24		

Apple-Cheese Melts

2 slices French or Italian bread, each 1 inch thick

2 tablespoons applesauce

1 medium apple, cored and cut into rings

2 ounces fat-free Cheddar cheese, sliced

2 ounces Gorgonzola cheese, crumbled

Set oven control to broil. Place bread on ungreased cookie sheet. Broil with tops about 4 inches from heat until golden brown; turn. Spread applesauce on bread slices. Place half of apple rings on each bread slice. Top with cheeses. Broil just until cheese begins to melt.

1 Sandwich:		% Daily Value:	
Calories	265	Vitamin A	10%
Calories from fat	80	Vitamin C	4%
Fat, g	9	Calcium	38%
Saturated, g	4	Iron	6%
Cholesterol, mg	20		
Sodium, mg	690		
Carbohydrate, g	33		
Dietary Fiber, g	3		
Protein, g	16		

Cheese Enchiladas

Photograph on page 70.

1/2 cup fat-free cottage cheese

1/2 cup shredded reduced-fat Monterey Jack or Cheddar cheese

1 small tomato, chopped (1/2 cup)

2 green onions, sliced

1 teaspoon chili powder

1/4 teaspoon salt

1 small clove garlic, finely chopped

4 corn tortillas (6 inches in diameter)

1/4 cup mild taco sauce

1/4 cup shredded reduced-fat Monterey Jack or Cheddar cheese

Heat oven to 375°. Spray two 14-ounce shallow oval casseroles or rectangular baking dish, 11×7×1 1/2 inches, with nonstick cooking spray. Mix cottage cheese, 1/2 cup Monterey Jack cheese, the tomato, onions, chili powder, salt and garlic. Spread about 1/3 cup of the cheese mixture on each tortilla. Roll up tortillas; place seam side down in casseroles. Spoon taco sauce over tortillas; sprinkle with 1/4 cup Monterey Jack cheese.

Bake uncovered 15 to 20 minutes or until hot and cheese is melted.

2 Enchiladas:		% Daily Value:	
Calories	295	Vitamin A	34%
Calories from fat	80	Vitamin C	20%
Fat, g	9	Calcium	48%
Saturated, g	5	Iron	8%
Cholesterol, mg	25		
Sodium, mg	990		
Carbohydrate, g	34		
Dietary Fiber, g	4		
Protein, g	23		

Sloppy Bean Josés

This Mexican cousin of a sloppy Joe is meatless and serves up a wonderful combination of sweet and spicy hot flavors. Serve it instead of a meat barbecue any time you'd like, from Cinco de Mayo to the Fourth of July!

1 teaspoon vegetable oil

1 medium onion, chopped (1/2 cup)

1 teaspoon chili powder

1 teaspoon fresh or 1/4 teaspoon dried oregano leaves, crushed

1/8 teaspoon ground cinnamon

Dash of red pepper sauce

2 tablespoons diced dried fruit and raisins

1 cup barbecued beans

2 French rolls or brat buns

Heat oil in 10-inch nonstick skillet over medium-high heat. Sauté onion in oil. Stir in chili powder, oregano, cinnamon and red pepper sauce. Cook until spices are browned, stirring constantly. Stir in fruit and beans. Cover and cook over medium-low heat 10 to 12 minutes or until flavors are blended. Cut a V-shaped wedge out of each roll; fill with bean mixture. Serve immediately.

1 Sandwich:		% Daily Value:	
Calories	255	Vitamin A	10%
Calories from fat	45	Vitamin C	14%
Fat, g	5	Calcium	8%
Saturated, g	1	Iron	20%
Cholesterol, mg	0		
Sodium, mg	720		
Carbohydrate, g	50		
Dietary Fiber, g	7		
Protein, g	9		

Deluxe Scrambled Egg Sandwich

1/2 cup fat-free cholesterol-free egg product or egg substitute

2 tablespoons low-fat milk

Dash of salt

Dash of pepper

1/8 teaspoon prepared mustard

2 slices fat-free Swiss cheese

4 slices bread, toasted

2 tablespoons fat-free mayonnaise or salad dressing

4 slices medium tomato

Mix egg product, milk, salt, pepper and mustard with hand beater until blended. Spray 8-inch non-stick skillet with nonstick cooking spray. Heat skillet over medium heat. Pour egg mixture into pan. As mixture begins to set at bottom and side, gently lift cooked portions with spatula so that thin, uncooked portion can flow to bottom. Avoid constant stirring. Cook egg mixture over medium heat 3 to 4 minutes, without stirring, or until eggs are thickened throughout but still moist. Place cheese on eggs; remove from heat and let stand 1 minute.

Spread toast with mayonnaise. Place half of cooked egg mixture on each of 2 slices toast on plates; top with tomato slices. Top with remaining slices toast.

1 Sandwich:		% Daily Value:	
Calories	205	Vitamin A	6%
Calories from fat	10	Vitamin C	4%
Fat, g	1	Calcium	44%
Saturated, g	1	Iron	16%
Cholesterol, mg	2		
Sodium, mg	860		
Carbohydrate, g	32		
Dietary Fiber, g	2		
Protein, g	19		

Black Bean Soup

1 can (14 1/2 ounces) reduced-sodium chicken or vegetable broth

1 can (15 ounces) black beans, rinsed and drained

1 teaspoon chili powder

1/2 teaspoon ground cumin

1/8 teaspoon crushed red pepper

1 clove garlic, finely chopped

1 jalapeño chile, finely chopped

1 medium onion, chopped (1/2 cup)

1 small carrot, sliced (1/4 cup)

1 medium stalk celery, chopped (1/2 cup)

2 tablespoons tequila, if desired

1/4 cup diced jicama

2 tablespoons shredded fat-free Cheddar cheese

1 small tomato, seeded and chopped

Heat all ingredients except jicama, cheese and tomato to boiling; reduce heat. Cover and simmer 1 hour. Place soup in blender or food processor. Cover and blend at medium-high speed, stopping blender occasionally to scrape sides, until smooth. Serve topped with jicama, cheese and tomato.

1 Serving:		% Daily Value:	
Calories	320	Vitamin A	72%
Calories from fat	20	Vitamin C	54%
Fat, g	2	Calcium	24%
Saturated, g	0	Iron	38%
Cholesterol, mg	2		
Sodium, mg	950		
Carbohydrate, g	71		
Dietary Fiber, g	19		
Protein, g	24		

Vegetarian Chili

1 teaspoon vegetable oil

1/2 cup chopped onion (1 medium)

1/4 cup chopped green bell pepper

1 small zucchini, cut into 1×1/4×1/4-inch
sticks (1 cup)

1 clove garlic, chopped

1 can (15 to 16 ounces) pinto beans, rinsed
and drained

1 can (14.5 ounces) salsa tomatoes with
diced green chilies, undrained

1 teaspoon chili powder

2 tablespoons fat-free sour cream, if desired

Chili powder, if desired

Heat oil in 2-quart nonstick saucepan over
medium-high heat. Sauté onion, bell pepper, zucchini and garlic in oil. Stir in beans, tomatoes and
chili powder. Cover and cook over low heat 20
minutes. Serve with sour cream, sprinkle with chili
powder.

1 Serving:		% Daily Value:	
Calories	325	Vitamin A	20%
Calories from fat	30	Vitamin C	46%
Fat, g	4	Calcium	18%
Saturated, g	1	Iron	40%
Cholesterol, mg	0		
Sodium, mg	860		
Carbohydrate, g	71		
Dietary Fiber, g	19		
Protein, g	21		

Cold Gazpacho Soup

1 cup tomato juice

2 tablespoons red wine vinegar

1/4 teaspoon sugar

1/4 teaspoon salt

Dash of reduced-sodium Worcestershire
sauce

2 medium tomatoes, chopped
(about 1 1/2 cups)

1/2 cucumber, peeled and chopped
(3/4 cup)

1/2 green bell pepper, chopped (1/2 cup)

2 tablespoons chopped onion

1 clove garlic, finely chopped

Chopped cilantro, if desired

Place all ingredients except cilantro in blender.
Cover and blend at medium-high speed, stopping
blender occasionally to scrape sides, until blended,
but still chunky. Pour into bowls; top with
cilantro.

1 Serving:		% Daily Value:	
Calories	75	Vitamin A	16%
Calories from fat	10	Vitamin C	54%
Fat, g	1	Calcium	2%
Saturated, g	0	Iron	8%
Cholesterol, mg	0		
Sodium, mg	720		
Carbohydrate, g	17		
Dietary Fiber, g	3		
Protein, g	3		

Vegetarian Chili

4

Two Meals from One

*Jamaican Turkey
(page 110),
Turkey–Brown Rice
Pilaf (page 111)*

Beef and Onion Fajitas

2 SERVINGS (2 FAJITAS PER SERVING)

1 tablespoon fat-free Italian dressing

1/2 medium green bell pepper, cut into 2×1/4-inch strips

1/2 small red onion, cut into thin strips

1/2 of sliced, cooked flank steak from Cajun Flank Steak with Lemon Rice (page 94)

4 warm whole wheat or low-fat flour tortillas (8 inches in diameter)*

1/2 cup reduced-sodium salsa

Fat-free sour cream, if desired

Cilantro, if desired

Heat Italian dressing in 10-inch nonstick skillet over medium-high heat. Cook bell pepper and onion in dressing about 2 minutes or until tender. Stir in beef. Cook 3 minutes, stirring constantly, until hot.

Serve beef filling with warm tortillas, salsa, sour cream and cilantro if desired. For each serving, place 1/4 of the beef filling, salsa, sour cream and cilantro in center of tortilla. Fold 1 end up 1 inch over filling; fold right and left sides over folded end.

*To warm tortillas: Heat oven to 350°. Wrap tortillas in aluminum foil. Heat 10 minutes. To microwave, wrap tortillas in paper towel and microwave on high 30 to 60 seconds.

2 Fajitas:		% Daily Value:	
Calories	340	Vitamin A	40%
Calories from fat	90	Vitamin C	34%
Fat, g	10	Calcium	6%
Saturated, g	3	Iron	24%
Cholesterol, mg	60		
Sodium, mg	935		
Carbohydrate, g	39		
Dietary Fiber, g	7		
Protein, g	30		

Cajun Flank Steak with Lemon Rice

1-pound flank steak

2 tablespoons Cajun seasoning blend for beef or pork

1/2 lemon, cut into wedges

Lemon Rice (below)

2 lemon wedges

Cilantro, if desired

Set oven to broil. Spray broiler pan with nonstick cooking spray. Cut both sides of beef steak in diamond pattern 1/8 inch deep. Rub seasoning blend on both sides of beef. Place on rack in broiler pan. Broil beef with top 2 to 3 inches from heat about 5 minutes or until seasoning is dark brown. (Move farther from heat if necessary.) Turn beef. Broil 5 minutes longer. Squeeze lemon over beef. Let stand 5 minutes. Cut beef across grain at slanted angle into thin slices. Reserve half the beef for Beef and Onion Fajitas (page 92). Serve remaining beef over Lemon Rice. Garnish with lemon wedges and cilantro.

Lemon Rice

1 1/3 cups water

2/3 cup long grain rice

1 teaspoon grated lemon peel

1/2 cup frozen peas

1/2 lemon, cut into wedges

Heat water, rice and lemon peel to boiling in 2-quart saucepan; reduce heat to low. Cover and cook 12 minutes. Stir in peas. Cook, uncovered, 2 to 4 minutes or until rice is tender and peas are hot.

1 Serving:		% Daily Value:	
Calories	415	Vitamin A	6%
Calories from fat	70	Vitamin C	10%
Fat, g	8	Calcium	4%
Saturated, g	3	Iron	26%
Cholesterol, mg	60		
Sodium, mg	320		
Carbohydrate, g	59		
Dietary Fiber, g	3		
Protein, g	30		

Barbecued Pepper-Beef Sandwiches

1/2 of cooked roast from Peppered Pot Roast au Jus (page 95)

1 teaspoon olive or vegetable oil

1 medium onion, chopped (1/2 cup)

1/3 cup chopped celery

1 tablespoon packed brown sugar

1 teaspoon reduced-sodium Worcestershire sauce

1 can (8 ounces) tomato sauce

2 large kaiser rolls, split

Shred beef. Heat oil in 1 1/2-quart saucepan over high heat. Sauté onion and celery in oil; reduce heat to medium-low. Stir in brown sugar, Worcestershire sauce, tomato sauce and beef. Cook, uncovered, 10 minutes, stirring occasionally. Serve on rolls.

1 Serving:		% Daily Value:	
Calories	415	Vitamin A	10%
Calories from fat	70	Vitamin C	14%
Fat, g	8	Calcium	8%
Saturated, g	3	Iron	28%
Cholesterol, mg	55		
Sodium, mg	1,190		
Carbohydrate, g	61		
Dietary Fiber, g	5		
Protein, g	30		

Peppered Pot Roast au Jus

Porcini mushrooms are valued for their rich, meaty flavor. In this twist on an old favorite, porcini mushrooms help create a delicious broth—spoon it liberally over the vegetables!

1-pound beef round rump or round tip roast

1 teaspoon coarse ground black pepper or lemon pepper

4 new potatoes (2 inches in diameter)

2 carrots, quartered

1 medium onion, quartered

1/2 cup boiling water

1/2 package (.5-ounce size) dried porcini mushrooms

1 teaspoon chopped fresh or 1/4 teaspoon dried thyme leaves

1 clove garlic, finely chopped

Heat oven to 325°. Heat 10-inch nonstick skillet over high heat. Sprinkle beef with pepper. Cook beef 5 minutes, turning several times, until evenly brown. Place in 2-quart casserole. Arrange potatoes, carrots and onion around beef. Pour water over beef and vegetables. Add mushrooms; submerge in liquid. Sprinkle thyme and garlic over top. Cover and bake 1 1/2 to 2 hours or until beef is tender. Let stand 10 minutes. Cut beef in half; reserve 1 half for Barbecued Pepper-Beef Sandwiches (page 94). Cut remaining beef into thin slices. Serve with vegetables and pan juices.

1 Serving:		% Daily Value:	
Calories	345	Vitamin A	100%
Calories from fat	35	Vitamin C	28%
Fat, g	4	Calcium	6%
Saturated, g	2	Iron	32%
Cholesterol, mg	55		
Sodium, mg	85		
Carbohydrate, g	58		
Dietary Fiber, g	7		
Protein, g	26		

BAKEWARE AND SUCH

If you don't already have some smaller baking dishes, you may want to purchase a few. Disposable aluminum bakeware is an option and can be found in most supermarkets. Look for small loaf pans, individual pie pans and six-cup muffin pans in particular. If you have a casserole or baking dish and don't know the the size, use liquid measuring cupfuls of water and fill it to the top. Make a note on a card taped to the inside of your cupboard as a reminder the next time you need to know. Some specific utensils you will want to have are:

- 8×8×2-inch or 9×9×2-inch square pan or baking dish

- 11×7×1 1/2-inch or 10×6 1/2-inch pan or baking dish

- 9×5×3-inch or 8 1/2×4 1/2×2 1/2-inch loaf pan

- 8- or 9-inch round pan

- 9×1 1/4-inch pie plate

- 1- and 1 1/2-quart casseroles

- Two 8-ounce and 10-ounce custard cups

- Two 16-ounce round or oval individual casseroles

- Two 4 1/2×1 1/4-inch tart pans

Zesty Beef Stroganoff

2 cooked beef tenderloin steaks from Tenderloin Steaks with Horseradish Gravy (page 98)

1 teaspoon vegetable oil

1 medium onion, cut into 2×1/4-inch strips (about 1/2 cup)

1/2 cup gravy from Tenderloin Steaks (page 98)

1 tablespoon tomato paste

4 ounces fresh mushrooms, sliced (about 1 1/2 cups)

1/4 cup fat-free sour cream

2 cups hot cooked rice or cholesterol-free noodles

Chopped parsley, if desired

Cut tenderloin steaks into 1/4-inch slices. Heat oil in 10-inch nonstick skillet over medium-high heat. Sauté onion in oil. Stir in beef, gravy, tomato paste and mushrooms; reduce heat to medium-low. Cover and cook 6 to 8 minutes or until hot. Just before serving, stir in sour cream. Serve over rice, sprinkle with parsley.

1 Serving:		% Daily Value:	
Calories	400	Vitamin A	6%
Calories from fat	80	Vitamin C	6%
Fat, g	9	Calcium	8%
Saturated, g	3	Iron	24%
Cholesterol, mg	55		
Sodium, mg	410		
Carbohydrate, g	56		
Dietary Fiber, g	2		
Protein, g	26		

Zesty Beef Stroganoff

Tenderloin Steaks with Horseradish Gravy

⧗ ◆ ♥ ▪

Beef tenderloin, often called filet mignon when cut into steaks, is one of the six lowest-fat cuts of beef. Here we've combined it with vegetables and a zippy horseradish gravy. Use your favorite au jus gravy mix in this flavorful recipe.

1/2 cup au jus natural-style gravy

2 tablespoons prepared horseradish

1/2 small zucchini or summer squash, cut into 2×1/4-inch strips (1/2 cup)

3 medium fresh mushrooms, sliced

1-pound beef tenderloin, cut into four 1-inch steaks

1/4 teaspoon salt

1/4 teaspoon pepper

1 medium tomato, cut into 6 wedges

Parsley sprigs, if desired

Heat oven to 350°. Spray square baking dish, 8×8×2 inches, with nonstick cooking spray. Mix gravy and horseradish in small bowl. Stir in zucchini and mushrooms.

Heat 10-inch nonstick skillet over high heat. Place beef steaks in skillet. Cook 1 minute on each side. (Beef will be rare.) Place in baking dish. Sprinkle with salt and pepper. Pour vegetable gravy over beef. Bake, uncovered, 15 minutes for medium rare or until desired degree of doneness. Reserve 2 beef steaks and 1/2 cup of the gravy for Zesty Beef Stroganoff (page 96). Place remaining steaks on platter; spoon vegetables on platter. Drizzle with remaining gravy. Garnish with tomato and parsley if desired.

1 Serving:		% Daily Value:	
Calories	180	Vitamin A	4%
Calories from fat	65	Vitamin C	12%
Fat, g	7	Calcium	2%
Saturated, g	3	Iron	16%
Cholesterol, mg	55		
Sodium, mg	340		
Carbohydrate, g	7		
Dietary Fiber, g	1		
Protein, g	23		

Slow-cooked Beef 'n Bean Bake

Dried beans are inexpensive, easy to store and packed with fiber. When you cook them slowly, you control the amount of sodium. Not only does this dish fill your kitchen with a tantalizing aroma, you also get two great meals!

1 teaspoon vegetable oil

1/2 pound lean beef round steak, cubed

1/4 teaspoon pepper

1/2 cup dried black-eyed peas, soaked,* rinsed and drained

1/4 cup dried kidney beans, soaked,* rinsed and drained

1 cup fat-free salt-free beef-flavored broth

1 tablespoon chopped fresh or 1 teaspoon dried oregano leaves

1 teaspoon chili powder

1 can (14 1/2 ounces) chunky salsa tomatoes

Heat oven to 325°. Heat oil in 10-inch ovenproof skillet over high heat. Sauté round steak in oil about 3 minutes or until brown. Sprinkle with pepper. Stir in remaining ingredients. Cook 3 minutes or until bubbly; cover. Place skillet in oven. Bake 1 1/2 to 2 hours or until beans are tender. Reserve 1 1/4 cups beef and bean mixture for Beef and Bean Tostadas (page 100). Serve remaining beef and bean mixture with reduced-sodium crackers if desired.

*To soak beans, place beans in 2 cups cold water. Let stand at room temperature 8 to 12 hours. To quick-soak beans, place beans in 2-quart saucepan. Add 2 cups water. Heat to boiling. Cook 2 minutes; remove from heat. Cover and let stand for 1 hour.

1 Serving:		% Daily Value:	
Calories	175	Vitamin A	8%
Calories from fat	35	Vitamin C	14%
Fat, g	4	Calcium	6%
Saturated, g	1	Iron	24%
Cholesterol, mg	30		
Sodium, mg	210		
Carbohydrate, g	25		
Dietary Fiber, g	10		
Protein, g	20		

Beef and Bean Tostada

Here is your second reward for slow-cooking the beef and beans—an easy, fast second meal with maximum home-cooked taste! This filling is also a great pita stuffer.

2 whole wheat or low-fat flour tortillas (8 inches in diameter)

1 1/4 cups beef and bean mixture from Slow-cooked Beef 'n Bean Bake (page 99)

1 medium tomato, chopped (about 3/4 cup)

1 cup grated fat-free Cheddar cheese (4 ounces)

Fat-free sour cream, if desired

Chopped fresh cilantro, if desired

Heat oven to 375°. Spray cookie sheet with non-stick cooking spray. Place tortillas on cookie sheet. Top with beef and bean mixture, tomato and cheese. Bake about 20 minutes or until hot. Cut into wedges. Top with sour cream and cilantro if desired.

1 Serving:		% Daily Value:	
Calories	341	Vitamin A	20%
Calories from fat	45	Vitamin C	24%
Fat, g	5	Calcium	48%
Saturated, g	8	Iron	32%
Cholesterol, mg	60		
Sodium, mg	670		
Carbohydrate, g	464		
Dietary Fiber, g	12		
Protein, g	408		

Beef and Bean Tostada

Marinated "Beefalo" Tips and Pasta

Here's a no-risk way to broaden your horizons. You won't be able to tell the difference between the beef and the buffalo, which are both used in this recipe. Buffalo has become available in many large grocery stores because it is lean, flavorful and plentiful now that it's bred commercially.

1/4 cup red wine vinegar

1 tablespoon packed brown sugar

1/4 teaspoon salt

1/2 teaspoon lemon pepper

1 1/2 teaspoons chopped fresh or
    1/2 teaspoon dried oregano leaves

3 cloves garlic, finely chopped

1 can (15 ounces) Italian-style tomato sauce

1/2 pound lean buffalo or venison round
    steak, cut into 3/4-inch cubes

1/2 pound lean beef round steak, cut into
    3/4-inch cubes

2 cups hot cooked cholesterol-free noodles
    or bow tie pasta (about 4 ounces)

Mix vinegar, brown sugar, salt, lemon pepper, oregano, garlic and tomato sauce in ungreased 2-quart casserole. Add meat. Cover and refrigerate at least 1 hour but not more than 24 hours.

Heat oven to 325°. Cover and bake 1 1/2 to 2 hours or until meat is tender. Reserve 1 cup "beefalo" mixture for Easy Chuckwagon Stew (right). Serve remaining beefalo mixture and sauce over pasta.

1 Serving:		% Daily Value:	
Calories	350	Vitamin A	6%
Calories from fat	35	Vitamin C	18%
Fat, g	4	Calcium	6%
Saturated, g	1	Iron	30%
Cholesterol, mg	65		
Sodium, mg	550		
Carbohydrate, g	53		
Dietary Fiber, g	3		
Protein, g	28		

Easy Chuckwagon Stew

1 cup "beefalo" mixture from Marinated
    "Beefalo" Tips and Pasta (left)

2 tablespoons pearl barley

2 cups frozen stew vegetables

1/4 cup shredded fat-free Cheddar cheese,
    if desired

Heat oven to 325°. Stir beefalo mixture, barley and vegetables in ungreased 1-quart casserole. Cover and bake 30 to 40 minutes or until barley is tender. Top servings with cheese if desired.

1 Serving:		% Daily Value:	
Calories	285	Vitamin A	85%
Calories from fat	25	Vitamin C	22%
Fat, g	3	Calcium	10%
Saturated, g	1	Iron	28%
Cholesterol, mg	65		
Sodium, mg	610		
Carbohydrate, g	46		
Dietary Fiber, g	10		
Protein, g	28		

Easy Chuckwagon Stew

Ginger Pork Medallions

1-pound pork tenderloin

2 tablespoons frozen (thawed) orange juice concentrate

1 tablespoon honey

1 tablespoon barbecue sauce

1/2 teaspoon soy sauce

1/4 teaspoon ground ginger

1 clove garlic, finely chopped

Cilantro leaves, if desired

Place pork tenderloin in ungreased shallow baking dish. Mix orange juice, honey, barbecue sauce, soy sauce, ginger and garlic until blended. Brush on pork, turning to coat both sides. Cover and refrigerate at least 1 hour but no longer than 12 hours.

Heat oven to 325°. Spray rack of shallow roasting pan with nonstick cooking spray. Remove pork from marinade; reserve marinade. Place pork on rack in roasting pan. Insert meat thermometer horizontally so tip is in center of thickest part of pork. Roast uncovered about 45 minutes, turning and brushing with marinade several times, until glazed or until thermometer registers 160°. Let stand 10 minutes. Slice pork into twelve 1/2-inch round medallions. Reserve 6 pork medallions for Caribbean Pork Kabobs (right). Serve remaining pork with cilantro if desired.

1 Serving:		% Daily Value:	
Calories	170	Vitamin A	*
Calories from fat	35	Vitamin C	10%
Fat, g	4	Calcium	*
Saturated, g	2	Iron	8%
Cholesterol, mg	65		
Sodium, mg	125		
Carbohydrate, g	9		
Dietary Fiber, g	0		
Protein, g	24		

Caribbean Pork Kabobs

6 cooked pork medallions from Ginger Pork Medallions (left)

1 can (8 ounces) pineapple chunks in unsweetened juice, drained with juice reserved

1/2 medium bell pepper, cut into 1-inch squares

4 large fresh mushroom caps, cut in half

1/8 teaspoon ground red pepper (cayenne)

1/2 teaspoon toasted or oriental sesame oil

2 cups hot cooked brown rice

2 lime wedges

Cut pork medallions into 1-inch chunks. Thread pork, pineapple, bell pepper and mushrooms, alternating ingredients, on four 8-inch skewers.* Mix 2 tablespoons reserved pineapple juice, red pepper and sesame oil until blended. Place kabobs in ungreased shallow baking dish. Pour pineapple marinade over kabobs. Cover and refrigerate at least 1 hour but no longer than 4 hours.

Set oven control to broil. Spray rack of broiler pan with nonstick cooking spray. Place kabobs on rack. Broil with tops 3 to 4 inches from heat 6 to 8 minutes, turning once and basting with marinade, until hot. Discard any remaining marinade. Place rice on plates; top with kabobs. Squeeze lime juice over kabobs and rice.

*If using bamboo or wooden skewers, soak in water 30 minutes before using to prevent burning.

1 Serving:		% Daily Value:	
Calories	435	Vitamin A	2%
Calories from fat	70	Vitamin C	36%
Fat, g	8	Calcium	4%
Saturated, g	2	Iron	16%
Cholesterol, mg	65		
Sodium, mg	135		
Carbohydrate, g	65		
Dietary Fiber, g	5		
Protein, g	31		

Chicken Enchilada Casserole

This easy casserole captures all the spice, color and delicious taste of traditional enchiladas, but with only about 1/3 of the fat!

Reserved cooked chicken from Easy Pepper-Jelly Chicken (page 106)

1 teaspoon vegetable oil

1 medium onion, chopped (1/2 cup)

1/2 red bell pepper, chopped

1/2 teaspoon chopped jalapeño pepper

1/4 teaspoon ground cumin

1 can (7 ounces) salsa verde (Mexican green sauce)

1/4 cup fat-free soft cream cheese

1/2 cup baked reduced-fat corn tortilla chips, coarsely broken

2 tablespoons reduced-sodium salsa

Cilantro, if desired

Heat oven to 375°. Spray 1-quart casserole with nonstick cooking spray. Shred chicken. Heat oil in 10-inch nonstick skillet over medium-high heat. Sauté onion in oil. Stir in bell pepper, jalapeño pepper and cumin. Cook 1 minute, stirring constantly. Add chicken and 1/2 cup salsa verde; reduce heat to medium-low. Cook, uncovered, 3 minutes. Stir in cream cheese until blended. Pour into casserole. Top with tortilla chips. Bake 20 minutes or until hot. Spoon remaining salsa verde and reduced-sodium salsa over top. Sprinkle with cilantro if desired.

1 Serving:		% Daily Value:	
Calories	370	Vitamin A	44%
Calories from fat	65	Vitamin C	84%
Fat, g	7	Calcium	4%
Saturated, g	1	Iron	20%
Cholesterol, mg	60		
Sodium, mg	460		
Carbohydrate, g	51		
Dietary Fiber, g	4		
Protein, g	30		

Easy Pepper-Jelly Chicken

1 pound skinless boneless chicken breasts or thighs, cut up

1/4 teaspoon salt

1 medium onion, cut into fourths

1 stalk celery, cut into fourths

2 red chilie peppers, cut lengthwise, ribs and seeds removed

Two 4-inch pieces lemon grass or strips lemon peel

3/4 cup uncooked acini di pepe macaroni

1/3 cup jalapeño jelly, melted

Place chicken in 3-quart saucepan; cover with water. Add salt, onion, celery, chilie peppers and lemon grass. Cover and heat to boiling; reduce heat to low. Simmer 1 hour or until chicken is very tender; remove chicken. Cover and refrigerate half the chicken for Chicken Enchilada Casserole (page 105).

Strain broth. Heat 2 cups broth to boiling in 1 1/2-quart saucepan. Stir in acini di pepe macaroni. Cook, uncovered, over medium-low heat 10 to 12 minutes or until tender; drain. Place pasta and remaining chicken on platter. Drizzle with jelly.

1 Serving:		% Daily Value:	
Calories	285	Vitamin A	*
Calories from fat	35	Vitamin C	2%
Fat, g	4	Calcium	2%
Saturated, g	1	Iron	10%
Cholesterol, mg	60		
Sodium, mg	70		
Carbohydrate, g	35		
Dietary Fiber, g	1		
Protein, g	28		

Curry Chicken Pie

When you just have to have a chicken pot pie, try our version that knocks about 100 calories off the traditional recipe and takes the fat down from 38 grams to only 13 grams. And, there's the bonus of the crunch from the crumb coating of Oven Crisp Chicken!

2 cooked chicken breast halves from Oven Crisp Chicken (page 108)

2 cups frozen (thawed) mixed vegetables

1/2 teaspoon curry powder

1 can (10 3/4 ounces) condensed reduced-fat cream of chicken soup

2/3 cup Bisquick Reduced Fat baking mix

1/3 cup low-fat milk

Heat oven to 425°. Spray two 2-cup round casseroles with nonstick cooking spray. Chop chicken breasts. Mix chicken, vegetables, curry powder and soup. Place half the chicken mixture in each casserole. Mix baking mix and milk; pour over chicken. Bake 20 to 25 minutes or until top is golden brown.

1 Serving:		% Daily Value:	
Calories	540	Vitamin A	94%
Calories from fat	115	Vitamin C	6%
Fat, g	13	Calcium	20%
Saturated, g	4	Iron	30%
Cholesterol, mg	75		
Sodium, mg	1,480		
Carbohydrate, g	76		
Dietary Fiber, g	9		
Protein, g	38		

Curry Chicken Pie

Black Bean–Chicken Chili

⬤ ♥ ▮ ⩔

Enjoy this fiesta for your taste buds, with only 7 grams of fat compared to 21 grams for traditional chili con carne! If you'd also like to decrease the sodium, try using cooked, dried black beans to which you have added no salt.

2 cooked chicken breast halves from Honey Mustard Chicken (page 110)

1 cup reduced-sodium chunky salsa

2 teaspoons chili powder

1/4 teaspoon salt

1/2 teaspoon ground cumin

1 can (15 ounces) black beans, rinsed and drained

1 can (8 ounces) tomato sauce

2 tablespoons lime fat-free yogurt

Chop chicken breasts. Heat remaining ingredients except yogurt in 2-quart saucepan over medium heat 15 minutes, stirring occasionally, until flavors are blended. Stir in chicken. Cook 5 minutes longer. Top servings with yogurt.

1 Serving:		% Daily Value:	
Calories	460	Vitamin A	92%
Calories from fat	65	Vitamin C	52%
Fat, g	7	Calcium	24%
Saturated, g	2	Iron	46%
Cholesterol, mg	60		
Sodium, mg	2,160		
Carbohydrate, g	73		
Dietary Fiber, g	20		
Protein, g	46		

Oven Crisp Chicken

⧗ ⬤ ♥ ▮

You have two great choices for the second half of this recipe. Make Curry Chicken Pie (page 106), or reheat in the microwave for a second meal. To reheat two pieces, microwave uncovered on high 1 to 1 1/2 minutes.

1/4 cup fat-free ranch dressing

3/4 cup reduced-fat crisp wheat cracker crumbs

1 tablespoon chopped fresh or 1 teaspoon dried thyme leaves

1 teaspoon paprika

4 skinless boneless chicken breast halves (about 1 pound)

Heat oven to 425°. Spray rack of broiler pan or baking dish with nonstick cooking spray. Pour dressing into small bowl. Mix cracker crumbs, thyme and paprika in separate small bowl or plastic bag. Dip chicken breasts into dressing; coat with crumb mixture. Place chicken on rack in pan. Bake 35 to 40 minutes or until golden brown and juices run clear. Cover and refrigerate 2 chicken breast halves for use in Curry Chicken Pie (page 106).

1 Serving:		% Daily Value:	
Calories	195	Vitamin A	4%
Calories from fat	45	Vitamin C	*
Fat, g	5	Calcium	2%
Saturated, g	1	Iron	8%
Cholesterol, mg	60		
Sodium, mg	330		
Carbohydrate, g	13		
Dietary Fiber, g	1		
Protein, g	26		

Oven Crisp Chicken, Sweet-and-Sour Cabbage Slaw (page 117)

Honey Mustard Chicken

1/2 teaspoon ground ginger

1/4 teaspoon ground coriander

1/2 teaspoon grated lime peel

4 skinless boneless chicken breast halves (about 1 pound)

2 tablespoons honey mustard

2 tablespoons lime juice

2 cups cooked seasoned rice and grain mixture, made without butter

1 green onion, sliced

Set oven control to broil. Spray broiler pan with nonstick cooking spray. Mix ginger, coriander and lime peel; rub seasonings on both sides of chicken breasts. Place chicken on rack in broiler pan; let stand 5 minutes. Mix mustard and lime juice; spread half over chicken. Broil chicken with tops 3 to 4 inches from heat 4 minutes; turn. Spread remaining mustard mixture over chicken. Broil 4 to 6 minutes longer or until juices run clear. Reserve 2 chicken breast halves for Black Bean–Chicken Chili (page 108). Serve remaining chicken over rice and grain mixture. Top with green onion.

1 Serving:		% Daily Value:	
Calories	385	Vitamin A	*
Calories from fat	45	Vitamin C	2%
Fat, g	5	Calcium	6%
Saturated, g	2	Iron	22%
Cholesterol, mg	65		
Sodium, mg	1,510		
Carbohydrate, g	53		
Dietary Fiber, g	1		
Protein, g	33		

Jamaican Turkey

Photograph on page 90.

1 teaspoon ground allspice

1 tablespoon chopped fresh or 1 teaspoon dried thyme leaves

1/4 teaspoon ground cinnamon

1/4 teaspoon ground nutmeg

1/4 teaspoon pepper

Dash of ground red pepper (cayenne)

1-pound turkey tenderloin

1 small onion, sliced

1/2 medium green bell pepper, sliced

1/4 cup mango chutney

Heat grill to medium. Spray 9-inch sheet of aluminum foil with nonstick cooking spray. Mix allspice, thyme, cinnamon, nutmeg, pepper and red pepper; rub seasonings on both sides of tenderloin. Place turkey on foil; top with onion and bell pepper. Cover with another 9-inch sheet of foil; fold edges together to seal packet.

Grill 4 inches from heat 20 minutes. Open packet. Remove turkey; keep vegetable mixture warm. Grill turkey 4 to 5 minutes longer or until brown and juice runs clear. Cut tenderloin in half. Reserve half the turkey for Turkey–Brown Rice Pilaf (page 111). Thinly slice remaining turkey. Top with vegetable mixture and chutney.

1 Serving:		% Daily Value:	
Calories	170	Vitamin A	2%
Calories from fat	25	Vitamin C	18%
Fat, g	3	Calcium	2%
Saturated, g	1	Iron	8%
Cholesterol, mg	55		
Sodium, mg	70		
Carbohydrate, g	16		
Dietary Fiber, g	2		
Protein, g	22		

Turkey–Brown Rice Pilaf

Photograph on page 90.

Reserved cooked turkey tenderloin from Jamaican Turkey (page 110)

2 teaspoons vegetable oil

2 cups cooked brown rice or bulgur

1 medium carrot, finely chopped (1/2 cup)

2 green onions, chopped

1 stalk celery, finely chopped (about 1/2 cup)

2 tablespoons reduced-sodium chicken broth

1 tablespoon grated reduced-fat Parmesan cheese blend

2 tablespoons chopped fresh parsley, if desired

Chop turkey tenderloin. Heat oil in 10-inch non-stick skillet over medium-high heat. Cook rice, carrot, onions and celery in oil 5 minutes, stirring constantly, or until vegetables are tender and rice is toasted light brown. Stir in broth and turkey; reduce heat to medium-low. Cover and cook 5 minutes, stirring occasionally, or until hot. Top with cheese and parsley if desired.

1 Serving:		% Daily Value:	
Calories	380	Vitamin A	44%
Calories from fat	90	Vitamin C	6%
Fat, g	10	Calcium	10%
Saturated, g	3	Iron	14%
Cholesterol, mg	55		
Sodium, mg	165		
Carbohydrate, g	50		
Dietary Fiber, g	5		
Protein, g	28		

SHOPPING SMART AND HEALTHY

Supermarkets are increasingly full of choices that include foods specifically packaged to meet the needs of smaller households and health-conscious consumers. Grocery shopping can be a pleasant experience when you follow these handy tips.

- Don't shop when you're hungry. Eat something nutritious, such as a banana or slice of whole-grain bread, before you go shopping.

- Shop stores where meats and produce can be purchased by the piece rather than only by the package. Or rewrap items into two-serving packages before refrigerating or freezing.

- When buying meat, look for lean cuts such as rounds and tenderloins. Many cuts of meat are now labeled with percentages of fat to help you choose the fat content you want.

- Purchase turkeys that are not self-basting; they don't have added fat and sodium.

- Select ground turkey breast or ground turkey labeled lean.

- Buy water-packed canned fish products, such as water-packed tuna or salmon, instead of products packed in oil.

- Choose whole-grain versions of breads, cereals, crackers, muffins, English muffins, rice and pasta.

- Use the deli or salad bar to purchase just enough cut-up vegetables and meats for casseroles and pasta salads.

5

Salads and Sides

Citrus-Pasta Salad (page 118),
Green Beans and Red Peppers
(page 119)

Raspberry-Yogurt Salad

3/4 cup boiling water

1/2 package (4-serving size) sugar-free raspberry-flavored gelatin (1 1/2 teaspoons)

1 container (6 ounces) raspberry fat-free yogurt

1/2 cup fresh or frozen (thawed and well drained) raspberries

Pour boiling water over gelatin in small bowl; stir until gelatin is dissolved. Stir in yogurt; gently stir in raspberries. Pour into two 8-ounce custard cups. Refrigerate about 2 hours or until set.

1 Serving:		% Daily Value:	
Calories	80	Vitamin A	8%
Calories from fat	0	Vitamin C	14%
Fat, g	0	Calcium	12%
Saturated, g	0	Iron	4%
Cholesterol, mg	0		
Sodium, mg	90		
Carbohydrate, g	15		
Dietary Fiber, g	0		
Protein, g	5		

Peanutty Apple Coleslaw

Apple adds zest to this easy colesalw. Your best bets for apples in this salad are Cortland, Empire, Paulared, Red Delicious, Jonathon or Winesap apples.

1/4 teaspoon salt

1 teaspoon lemon juice

2 teaspoons reduced-fat peanut butter

2 teaspoons fat-free mayonnaise or salad dressing

2 to 3 teaspoons water

1 cup coleslaw mixture or shredded cabbage

1/2 crisp red apple, cut into 1 1/2×1/4×1/4-inch pieces

1 teaspoon chopped dry-roasted peanuts

Mix salt, lemon juice, peanut butter and mayonnaise with whisk in medium bowl until blended. Stir in water to desired consistency. Add coleslaw mixture and apple; toss. Sprinkle with peanuts just before serving.

1 Serving:		% Daily Value:	
Calories	65	Vitamin A	*
Calories from fat	25	Vitamin C	22%
Fat, g	3	Calcium	2%
Saturated, g	0	Iron	2%
Cholesterol, mg	0		
Sodium, mg	370		
Carbohydrate, g	10		
Dietary Fiber, g	2		
Protein, g	2		

Peanutty Apple Coleslaw, Crispy Cracked Wheat Taters (page 126)

Curried Artichoke Salad

Using only part of a package of frozen vegetables? Partially defrost vegetables in the refrigerator, then break or cut off what you need and return the rest to the freezer. Hot Artichoke Appetizer (page 36) is a great way to use the leftover artichokes from this salad.

1 1/2 cups fresh or frozen cauliflower flowerets

1/2 package (9-ounce size) frozen artichoke hearts

1/4 cup fat-free mayonnaise or salad dressing

1 tablespoon lemon juice

1/4 teaspoon curry powder

2 tablespoons chopped red bell pepper

Heat 1 inch water to boiling in 1 1/2-quart saucepan. Add cauliflower. Cover and heat to boiling; reduce heat. Boil 5 minutes. Stir in artichoke hearts. Cover and cook 5 to 7 minutes longer, stirring occasionally and separating artichokes with fork, until vegetables are tender. Drain well. Cool 10 minutes. Mix mayonnaise, lemon juice and curry powder. Toss vegetables with dressing and bell pepper. Serve warm or chilled.

1 Serving:		% Daily Value:	
Calories	80	Vitamin A	4%
Calories from fat	0	Vitamin C	94%
Fat, g	0	Calcium	6%
Saturated, g	0	Iron	8%
Cholesterol, mg	0		
Sodium, mg	480		
Carbohydrate, g	20		
Dietary Fiber, g	4		
Protein, g	4		

Teriyaki Spinach Salad

1 tablespoon stir-fry sauce with garlic and ginger

1 teaspoon teriyaki sauce

1 teaspoon sweet-and-sour sauce

4 cups fresh spinach leaves (3 ounces)

2/3 cup canned baby corn, rinsed and drained

1/2 cup sliced mushrooms

1 roma (plum) tomato, chopped

1 tablespoon bacon-flavored bits

Heat stir-fry, teriyaki and sweet-and-sour sauces in 10-inch skillet over medium heat, stirring constantly, about 1 minute or until hot and bubbly. Add spinach, baby corn and mushrooms. Toss vegetables with dressing for about 1 minute or until well coated and spinach is wilted. Remove from heat; sprinkle with tomato and bacon-flavored bits.

1 Serving:		% Daily Value:	
Calories	115	Vitamin A	98%
Calories from fat	20	Vitamin C	38%
Fat, g	2	Calcium	12%
Saturated, g	0	Iron	24%
Cholesterol, mg	0		
Sodium, mg	800		
Carbohydrate, g	21		
Dietary Fiber, g	5		
Protein, g	8		

Sweet-and-Sour Cabbage Slaw

Photograph on page 109.

2 tablespoons honey

2 tablespoons peach or apricot spreadable fruit

2 teaspoons cider vinegar

2 cups coleslaw mixture or shredded cabbage

2 green onions, sliced

1 medium carrot, shredded (2/3 cup)

Mix honey, spreadable fruit and vinegar in medium bowl. Add remaining ingredients; toss.

1 Serving:		% Daily Value:	
Calories	145	Vitamin A	56%
Calories from fat	0	Vitamin C	50%
Fat, g	0	Calcium	6%
Saturated, g	0	Iron	6%
Cholesterol, mg	0		
Sodium, mg	30		
Carbohydrate, g	38		
Dietary Fiber, g	4		
Protein, g	2		

Marinated Broccoli and Carrot Salad

1 1/2 cups broccoli flowerets

1/4 cup sliced carrot

1 large green onion, sliced

3 tablespoons fat-free Italian dressing

2 lettuce leaves

Heat 1 inch water to boiling in 1 1/2-quart saucepan. Add broccoli, carrot and onion. Cover and heat to boiling; reduce heat. Boil 10 to 12 minutes or until broccoli is crisp-tender; drain. Toss vegetables with dressing. Cover and refrigerate about 1 hour or until chilled. Serve on lettuce leaves.

1 Serving:		% Daily Value:	
Calories	25	Vitamin A	32%
Calories from fat	0	Vitamin C	56%
Fat, g	0	Calcium	4%
Saturated, g	0	Iron	4%
Cholesterol, mg	0		
Sodium, mg	200		
Carbohydrate, g	7		
Dietary Fiber, g	3		
Protein, g	2		

Southwestern Corn Salad

Photograph on page 70.

3/4 cup spicy reduced-sodium vegetable juice

1/4 teaspoon chili powder

1/4 teaspoon ground cumin

1 1/2 cups frozen corn

1 small zucchini, cut into 1×1/4×1/4-inch sticks (1/2 cup)

1/4 teaspoon salt

2 lettuce leaves, if desired

Juice from 1/2 lime (about 2 teaspoons)

Heat vegetable juice, chili powder and cumin in 1 1/2-quart saucepan to boiling. Stir in corn and zucchini. Cover and cook over medium heat 3 to 5 minutes, stirring occasionally, until vegetables are tender. Stir in salt. Cover and refrigerate about 2 hours or until chilled. Serve salad on lettuce leaves if desired. Drizzle with lime juice.

1 Serving:		% Daily Value:	
Calories	115	Vitamin A	16%
Calories from fat	0	Vitamin C	28%
Fat, g	0	Calcium	2%
Saturated, g	0	Iron	6%
Cholesterol, mg	0		
Sodium, mg	300		
Carbohydrate, g	30		
Dietary Fiber, g	5		
Protein, g	4		

Citrus-Pasta Salad

Photograph on page 112.

1/4 cup fat-free mayonnaise or salad dressing

1 tablespoon orange juice

1 teaspoon grated orange peel

1/4 teaspoon salt

3/4 cup cooked medium pasta shells

2 large radishes, sliced

1 orange, peeled, seeded and sectioned

1 package (10 ounces) broccoli cuts, thawed

Mix mayonnaise, orange juice, orange peel and salt in 2-quart bowl. Stir in pasta, radishes, orange sections and broccoli. Cover and chill at least 1 hour.

1 Serving:		% Daily Value:	
Calories	160	Vitamin A	26%
Calories from fat	10	Vitamin C	100%
Fat, g	1	Calcium	10%
Saturated, g	0	Iron	8%
Cholesterol, mg	0		
Sodium, mg	680		
Carbohydrate, g	37		
Dietary Fiber, g	6		
Protein, g	7		

Asparagus Parmesan

1 1/3 cups frozen cut asparagus

6 mushrooms, thinly sliced

2 teaspoons margarine or butter

1/8 teaspoon garlic powder

Freshly ground pepper

1 tablespoon grated reduced-fat Parmesan
cheese blend

Cook asparagus as directed on package—except
add mushrooms during last minute of cooking;
drain. Stir in remaining ingredients.

1 Serving:		% Daily Value:	
Calories	75	Vitamin A	10%
Calories from fat	45	Vitamin C	16%
Fat, g	5	Calcium	6%
Saturated, g	0	Iron	6%
Cholesterol, mg	2		
Sodium, mg	95		
Carbohydrate, g	6		
Dietary Fiber, g	2		
Protein, g	4		

Green Beans and Red Peppers

Photograph on page 112.

1/2 pound fresh green beans, broken into
2-inch pieces (2 cups)

1/2 medium red bell pepper, cut into
2×1/4-inch strips

1 tablespoon honey mustard

Place beans in 1 inch water in 1 1/2-quart
saucepan. Heat to boiling; reduce heat. Boil,
uncovered, 5 minutes. Cover and boil 5 to 10 minutes longer or until beans are crisp-tender; drain.
Stir in bell pepper and honey mustard.

1 Serving:		% Daily Value:	
Calories	35	Vitamin A	16%
Calories from fat	10	Vitamin C	36%
Fat, g	1	Calcium	6%
Saturated, g	0	Iron	6%
Cholesterol, mg	0		
Sodium, mg	110		
Carbohydrate, g	8		
Dietary Fiber, g	3		
Protein, g	2		

Creamy Cabbage

3 cups coleslaw mixture or shredded
    cabbage
1/4 cup fat-free cream cheese, softened
1/4 teaspoon celery seed
1/4 teaspoon celery salt
Dash of garlic powder
Freshly ground pepper
1 tablespoon plus 1 teaspoon milk

Heat 1/2 inch water to boiling in 1 1/2-quart
saucepan. Add coleslaw mixture. Cover and heat to
boiling; reduce heat. Boil 5 to 8 minutes or until
cabbage is crisp-tender; drain. Mix remaining
ingredients. Stir cream cheese mixture into hot
cabbage.

1 Serving:		% Daily Value:	
Calories	55	Vitamin A	2%
Calories from fat	10	Vitamin C	28%
Fat, g	1	Calcium	10%
Saturated, g	0	Iron	4%
Cholesterol, mg	0		
Sodium, mg	390		
Carbohydrate, g	8		
Dietary Fiber, g	2		
Protein, g	6		

Gingered Carrots

1/3 cup reduced-sodium chicken broth
2 teaspoons honey
1 teaspoon lime juice
2 slices fresh gingerroot, 1/8 inch thick
1 clove garlic, finely chopped
1/2 pound baby carrots (about 20)
1 green onion, sliced

Stir broth, honey, lime juice, gingerroot and garlic
in 1-quart saucepan. Add carrots. Cover and heat
to boiling; reduce heat to medium-low. Cook
8 minutes or until carrots are crisp-tender. Remove
and discard gingerroot. Cook, uncovered, over
medium-high heat 2 minutes or until liquid
is reduced by half. Sprinkle onion over carrots.

1 Serving:		% Daily Value:	
Calories	65	Vitamin A	100%
Calories from fat	0	Vitamin C	10%
Fat, g	0	Calcium	4%
Saturated, g	0	Iron	4%
Cholesterol, mg	0		
Sodium, mg	110		
Carbohydrate, g	18		
Dietary Fiber, g	3		
Protein, g	1		

Carrot-Potato Patties

2 SERVINGS (TWO 4-INCH PATTIES EACH)

1 1/2 medium carrots, shredded (1 cup)

1 medium potato, peeled and shredded (1 cup)

2 tablespoons grated onion

1/2 teaspoon salt

1/4 cup fat-free egg product or 2 egg whites

1/4 cup unsweetened applesauce

Mix all ingredients, except applesauce, in medium bowl. Spray nonstick griddle or 10-inch skillet with nonstick cooking spray. Heat griddle over medium heat or to 375°. For each patty, spoon approximately 1/2 cup batter onto hot griddle. Cook 2 to 3 minutes on each side or until golden brown. Top warm patties with applesauce.

1 Serving:		% Daily Value:	
Calories	95	Vitamin A	86%
Calories from fat	0	Vitamin C	8%
Fat, g	0	Calcium	2%
Saturated, g	0	Iron	6%
Cholesterol, mg	0		
Sodium, mg	600		
Carbohydrate, g	23		
Dietary Fiber, g	3		
Protein, g	4		

Peppery Corn and Tomatoes

1 1/3 cups frozen whole kernel corn

1/4 teaspoon garlic salt

Dash of ground red pepper (cayenne)

2 teaspoons margarine or butter

2 green onions, chopped

1/2 medium tomato, chopped

Cook corn as directed on package; drain. Stir in remaining ingredients.

1 Serving:		% Daily Value:	
Calories	130	Vitamin A	10%
Calories from fat	35	Vitamin C	18%
Fat, g	4	Calcium	2%
Saturated, g	1	Iron	4%
Cholesterol, mg	0		
Sodium, mg	175		
Carbohydrate, g	24		
Dietary Fiber, g	4		
Protein, g	3		

VEGGIE VITAMINS

Remember that important vitamins found in vegetables can be destroyed by overcooking or lost entirely by being cooked in too much water. Aim for a crisp-tender texture by cooking for only a short period of time, and cook in as little water as possible. To gain the benefit of vitamins that dissolve into cooking liquids, use the leftover liquid in creative ways; add it to soups, stews and sauces, or use it for basting meats.

Mushrooms in Wine

2 tablespoons dry white wine

1 teaspoon cornstarch

2 teaspoons margarine or butter

8 ounces mushrooms, cut in half (3 cups)

1 small clove garlic, finely chopped

1/8 teaspoon salt

Chopped fresh parsley, if desired

Mix wine and cornstarch. Heat margarine in 10-inch nonstick skillet over medium-high heat. Sauté mushrooms and garlic in margarine. Stir in cornstarch mixture and salt. Cook and stir 1 minute. Sprinkle servings with parsley if desired.

1 Serving:		% Daily Value:	
Calories	70	Vitamin A	4%
Calories from fat	35	Vitamin C	2%
Fat, g	4	Calcium	*
Saturated, g	1	Iron	8%
Cholesterol, mg	0		
Sodium, mg	190		
Carbohydrate, g	7		
Dietary Fiber, g	1		
Protein, g	2		

Buttercup Squash with Apples

1 small buttercup or other winter squash, cut in half, seeds and fibers removed (1 pound)

1/2 cup chopped tart apple

2 teaspoons packed brown sugar

2 teaspoons margarine or butter, softened

1/2 teaspoon lemon juice

Dash of ground nutmeg

Heat oven to 400°. Place squash halves cut sides up in ungreased rectangular baking dish, 11×7×1 1/2 inches. Mix remaining ingredients; spoon into squash. Cover and bake 30 to 40 minutes or until squash is tender.

1 Serving:		% Daily Value:	
Calories	130	Vitamin A	66%
Calories from fat	45	Vitamin C	14%
Fat, g	5	Calcium	2%
Saturated, g	1	Iron	4%
Cholesterol, mg	0		
Sodium, mg	50		
Carbohydrate, g	25		
Dietary Fiber, g	5		
Protein, g	1		

Buttercup Squash with Apples

Grilled Vegetable Kabobs

These flavorful veggies work equally well under the broiler, too.

1 teaspoon taco seasoning mix

1/4 cup fat-free Italian dressing

2 medium new potatoes, cut in half (1 to 1 1/2 inches in diameter)

1 small zucchini, cut in fourths

1 ear corn, cob broken or cut in fourths

1/2 bell pepper, cut in fourths

Heat grill. Mix taco seasoning and dressing. Thread remaining ingredients, alternating vegetables, on two 10-inch skewers, leaving space between pieces.* Brush dressing mixture over vegetables. Cover and grill kabobs over medium coals 4 inches from heat 25 to 30 minutes, turning frequently and brushing with dressing, until vegetables are tender.

*If using bamboo or wooden skewers, soak in water for 30 minutes before using to prevent burning.

1 Serving:		% Daily Value:	
Calories	180	Vitamin A	6%
Calories from fat	0	Vitamin C	34%
Fat, g	0	Calcium	2%
Saturated, g	0	Iron	12%
Cholesterol, mg	0		
Sodium, mg	330		
Carbohydrate, g	46		
Dietary Fiber, g	6		
Protein, g	5		

Roasted Fall Vegetables

Roasting vegetables at a high temperature intensifies their flavors, and produces a crisp, dry surface. For a fresh, moist look, drizzle with additional salad dressing just before serving.

4 ounces baby carrots, cut lengthwise in half (3/4 cup)

6 ounces butternut or acorn squash, cut into 3/4-inch cubes (1/2 cup)

1/2-pound leek, cut into pieces (1/2 cup)

5 small new potatoes, cut into 1-inch chunks (1/2 pound)

2 tablespoons fat-free honey-mustard dressing

2 teaspoons grated reduced-fat Parmesan cheese blend

Heat oven to 450°. Line jelly roll pan, 15 1/2× 10 1/2×1 inch, with aluminum foil. Spray foil with nonstick cooking spray. Mix carrots, squash, leek and potatoes with dressing until evenly coated. Place vegetables in a single layer on foil. Sprinkle with cheese. Roast 20 minutes or until vegetables are tender.

1 Serving:		% Daily Value:	
Calories	270	Vitamin A	84%
Calories from fat	0	Vitamin C	34%
Fat, g	0	Calcium	8%
Saturated, g	0	Iron	20%
Cholesterol, mg	0		
Sodium, mg	150		
Carbohydrate, g	68		
Dietary Fiber, g	7		
Protein, g	7		

Very Veggie

Vegetables are naturally low-calorie, lowfat and cholesterol-free. Those facts combined with the almost year-round availability of vegetables that once were seasonal and the resurgence of farmers' markets make vegetables an easy choice for filling out a healthy meal.

- Take advantage of seasonal fresh vegetable specials at the supermarket or the farmers' market. Avoid vegetables with bruises or soft spots.

- Purchase enough vegetables for two and ask how to prepare them. Make a note of those you like and dislike, but try them prepared at least two different ways before you make a final judgment.

- Many frozen vegetables come conveniently packaged for two. A 10-ounce package makes two or three servings. Buying the bags of individually quick frozen vegetables allows you to remove as much as is needed at a time.

- Frozen vegetables are an easy addition to cold pasta salads as they need only be thawed, not cooked. Try some of the many combinations of mixed vegetables available.

- For variety, mix vegetables with rice or couscous as a side dish rather than eating each separately.

- Add herbs and seasonings to plain vegetables or toss with bottled fat-free salad dressings for a different twist.

Italian Potato Fingers

1 pound large baking potatoes (about 2)

1 tablespoon fat-free Italian dressing

1 teaspoon olive or vegetable oil

1 teaspoon grated reduced-fat Italian cheese blend

1/2 cup reduced-sodium spaghetti sauce or salsa

Heat oven to 400°. Spray jelly roll pan, 15 1/2× 10 1/2×1 inch, with nonstick cooking spray. Cut potatoes lengthwise into 6 wedges; place in pan. Mix dressing and oil until blended. Brush potatoes with dressing mixture. Sprinkle with cheese. Bake 35 to 40 minutes or until potatoes are tender. Heat spaghetti sauce. Serve potatoes with spaghetti sauce dip.

1 Serving:		% Daily Value:	
Calories	235	Vitamin A	8%
Calories from fat	25	Vitamin C	30%
Fat, g	3	Calcium	4%
Saturated, g	0	Iron	16%
Cholesterol, mg	0		
Sodium, mg	105		
Carbohydrate, g	52		
Dietary Fiber, g	5		
Protein, g	5		

Crispy Cracked Wheat Taters

Photograph on page 115.

1/4 cup uncooked cracked wheat*

1/2 teaspoon vegetable oil

1 medium onion, chopped (1/3 cup)

1/2 teaspoon salt-free onion and herb seasoning blend

1 cup mashed potatoes

3 tablespoons grated reduced-fat Parmesan cheese blend

Heat 3/4 cup water to boiling in 1-quart saucepan. Add cracked wheat. Reduce heat to low. Cover and cook 20 minutes. Let stand, covered, 10 minutes.

Heat oven to 350°. Spray cookie sheet with non-stick cooking spray. Heat oil in 2-quart saucepan over medium-high heat. Cook onion and seasoning blend in oil until onions are tender. Stir in cracked wheat, potatoes and cheese. Drop 20 tablespoonfuls into 1 1/2-inch mounds about 1 inch apart on cookie sheet. Bake 20 to 25 minutes or until light brown.

*1/4 cup finely ground bulgur, soaked in 1/2 cup boiling water, may be substituted for the cooked cracked wheat. Let bulgur stand in boiling water, uncovered, 10 to 15 minutes or until water is absorbed. Fluff with fork.

1 Serving:		% Daily Value:	
Calories	185	Vitamin A	8%
Calories from fat	80	Vitamin C	6%
Fat, g	9	Calcium	14%
Saturated, g	3	Iron	2%
Cholesterol, mg	5		
Sodium, mg	360		
Carbohydrate, g	22		
Dietary Fiber, g	2		
Protein, g	6		

Potato-breaded Baked Veggies

Looking for an appealing new vegetable dish to serve with hamburgers? Then try these easy vegetables.

1/4 cup fat-free egg product or 2 egg whites

1/4 cup mashed potato mix

1 tablespoon grated reduced-fat Parmesan cheese blend

1/8 teaspoon garlic powder

1 tablespoon margarine, melted

12 fresh broccoli flowerets (about 2 cups)

1 medium red bell pepper, cut into 2×1/2-inch pieces

1/4 cup fat-free peppercorn ranch dressing, if desired

Heat oven to 400°. Line jelly roll pan, 15 1/2× 10 1/2×1 inch, with aluminum foil. Spray foil with nonstick cooking spray. Beat egg product slightly in small bowl. Mix potato buds, cheese, garlic powder and margarine in separate small bowl until crumbly. Dip vegetables into egg product; coat with potato mixture. Place vegetable pieces 1 inch apart on pan. Bake 20 to 25 minutes or until coating is golden brown and vegetables are tender. Serve with ranch dressing dip if desired.

1 Serving:		% Daily Value:	
Calories	125	Vitamin A	40%
Calories from fat	45	Vitamin C	100%
Fat, g	5	Calcium	8%
Saturated, g	1	Iron	8%
Cholesterol, mg	2		
Sodium, mg	180		
Carbohydrate, g	12		
Dietary Fiber, g	3		
Protein, g	6		

Parmesan Sweet Potato Rounds

1/4 cup reduced-sodium chicken broth

2 medium sweet potatoes or yams, peeled and cut into 1/4-inch slices (2 cups)

2 tablespoons grated reduced-fat Parmesan cheese blend

1 1/2 teaspoons fresh or 1/2 teaspoon dried thyme leaves

Heat oven to 375°. Spray pie plate, 9×1 1/4 inches, with nonstick cooking spray. Pour broth into pie plate. Place potato slices in an overlapping double layer over broth in pie plate. Sprinkle cheese and thyme evenly over potatoes. Cover with aluminum foil. Bake 30 minutes; remove foil. Bake 12 to 15 minutes longer or until potatoes are tender and broth is absorbed.

1 Serving:		% Daily Value:	
Calories	125	Vitamin A	100%
Calories from fat	10	Vitamin C	22%
Fat, g	1	Calcium	10%
Saturated, g	0	Iron	4%
Cholesterol, mg	2		
Sodium, mg	160		
Carbohydrate, g	28		
Dietary Fiber, g	3		
Protein, g	4		

Hawaiian Yam Casserole

2 medium sweet potatoes or yams, peeled and cut into 1/2-inch slices (about 2 cups)

1 can (8 ounces) crushed pineapple in juice, undrained

1 tablespoon packed brown sugar

2 tablespoons chopped pecans

1 tablespoon chopped crystallized ginger

1 teaspoon margarine

Heat oven to 375°. Spray 1-quart casserole with nonstick cooking spray. Layer yams and crushed pineapple in casserole. Sprinkle brown sugar, pecans and crystallized ginger over top; dot with margarine. Cover and bake about 45 minutes or until yams are tender.

1 Serving:		% Daily Value:	
Calories	290	Vitamin A	100%
Calories from fat	65	Vitamin C	30%
Fat, g	7	Calcium	6%
Saturated, g	1	Iron	6%
Cholesterol, mg	0		
Sodium, mg	40		
Carbohydrate, g	59		
Dietary Fiber, g	5		
Protein, g	3		

Hawaiian Yam Casserole

Spicy Brown Rice Veracruz

This spicy brown rice dish can also double as the main dish in a meatless meal. Serve it in half of a baked acorn squash, topped with a small jalapeño chile. Add a piece of corn bread and a glass of low-fat milk.

1 teaspoon vegetable oil

3/4 cup instant brown rice

1 medium onion, chopped (1/2 cup)

2 cloves garlic, finely chopped

1 can (10 ounces) diced tomatoes with green chilies, undrained

1 can (8 ounces) tomato sauce

1/2 teaspoon chopped fresh jalapeño chilies, if desired

Heat oil in 10-inch nonstick skillet over medium-high heat. Cook rice, onion and garlic in oil 4 to 5 minutes, stirring frequently, until rice is toasted. Stir in remaining ingredients. Cover and cook over medium-low heat 15 minutes or until rice is tender.

1 Serving:		% Daily Value:	
Calories	335	Vitamin A	20%
Calories from fat	45	Vitamin C	32%
Fat, g	5	Calcium	8%
Saturated, g	1	Iron	16%
Cholesterol, mg	0		
Sodium, mg	930		
Carbohydrate, g	72		
Dietary Fiber, g	8		
Protein, g	9		

RICE IS NICE

Rice is the most common of the grains on the market today. Try some of the flavored rices for variety, but read labels for sodium and fat content. Here are general guidelines for cooking rice; follow package directions for cooking method and amounts.

- General guidelines for cooking rice:
  1. Heat rice, water and salt (if desired) to boiling in 1- to 1 1/2-quart saucepan.
  2. Reduce heat; cover and cook the specified amount of time. Fluff with fork and steam 5 to 10 minutes.

Type rice	Time (minutes)	Yield per 1/2 cup/uncooked
Regular	15	1 1/2 cups
Parboiled (converted)	20 to 25	2 cups
Precooked (instant)	5	1 cup
Brown	50	2 cups
Wild	75 to 90	1 1/2 cups

- Cooked rice can be stored tightly covered in the refrigerator for up to five days or frozen in a covered container for up to six months. To reheat, tightly cover and microwave on high about 1 minute per cup. Or place rice in heavy saucepan and add 2 tablespoons water per cup of cooked rice. Cover and cook over low heat about 5 minutes.

- The shorter the rice grain, the stickier the rice. Medium grain rice works better than long grain rice in puddings because of its creamier characteristics.

Couscous Pilaf

3 SERVINGS (ABOUT 1 CUP EACH)

This flavorful medley makes three side-dish servings or two meatless main-dish servings.

3/4 cup uncooked couscous

1 cup reduced-sodium chicken broth

1 tablespoon margarine or butter

3 ounces fresh mushrooms, chopped (1/2 cup)

1/4 cup chopped cashews or pecans

1/3 cup chopped green bell pepper

1 medium tomato, chopped (2/3 cup)

1/2 teaspoon ground nutmeg

1/2 teaspoon ground coriander

1/2 teaspoon garlic salt

2 green onions, chopped

Heat oven to 375°. Spray round nonstick baking pan, 9×1 1/2 inches, or square baking dish, 8×8×2 inches, with nonstick cooking spray. Mix couscous and broth in pan; cover with aluminum foil. Bake 10 minutes; fluff with fork.

Meanwhile, heat margarine in 10-inch nonstick skillet over medium-high heat. Sauté mushrooms, cashews and bell pepper in margarine; remove from heat. Stir in remaining ingredients. Stir vegetable mixture into couscous in pan. Bake, uncovered, 10 minutes longer or until couscous is slightly brown.

1 Cup:		% Daily Value:	
Calories	285	Vitamin A	8%
Calories from fat	90	Vitamin C	18%
Fat, g	10	Calcium	2%
Saturated, g	2	Iron	8%
Cholesterol, mg	0		
Sodium, mg	430		
Carbohydrate, g	43		
Dietary Fiber, g	3		
Protein, g	9		

Poppy Seed Fettuccine

4 ounces uncooked fettuccine

2 teaspoons margarine or butter

1/4 teaspoon poppy seeds

Cook fettuccine as directed on package; drain. Stir in margarine and poppy seeds.

1 Serving:		% Daily Value:	
Calories	220	Vitamin A	6%
Calories from fat	55	Vitamin C	*
Fat, g	6	Calcium	2%
Saturated, g	1	Iron	12%
Cholesterol, mg	50		
Sodium, mg	55		
Carbohydrate, g	37		
Dietary Fiber, g	2		
Protein, g	7		

Eating for Good Health

Taking responsibility for your health by choosing nutritious food is the basis of healthy eating. It's a wise step to take whether you're trying to reduce your risk of diseases affected by diet, or working to manage a chronic condition you or a member of your family already have. In this chapter, we give you the information you need to eat healthfully and to reduce your risk for developing, or to learn to manage, some of the major illnesses common today. And, you won't have to give up great taste!

Just a reminder to our readers: This cookbook provides some general eating principles and food preparation guidelines that may help some individuals manage or reduce the risk of certain diseases. It is not designed to replace the individualized care or advice of your physician but rather to supplement it. For more information about these diseases or others that are not included in this book, please consult your physician.

Coronary Heart Disease

Coronary heart disease (CHD) is characterized by a buildup of fatty, cholesterol-filled deposits in the arteries, which can eventually clog them, block the flow of blood and cause a heart attack.

The condition is caused by a variety of factors, some beyond our control. For example, your risks for CHD are greater if you have a family history of the disease, are male or are older. The risks have an additive effect. If you're male and over age 50 and one of your parents or a sibling suffers from the disease, your chances of developing CHD become greater.

Fortunately, several risk factors for the disease remain within our control. Cigarette smoking is considered the most significant modifiable risk. Other modifiable risk factors include high blood pressure, high blood cholesterol, obesity and physical inactivity.

Eating strategies to reduce or manage risks for CHD focus on a low-fat, low-cholesterol diet. Your daily diet should not exceed 30 percent of calories from fat, with no more than 10 percent of those calories coming from saturated fat. These levels may be more strict for people who are already managing CHD. And it's advised that you limit cholesterol intake to no more than 300 milligrams per day.

Tips for Reducing Risk and Managing Heart Disease

- If you smoke, stop.

- Follow your doctor's advice for controlling high blood pressure.

- Eat a diet low in fat and cholesterol that contains plenty of whole-grain cereals and breads, fruits and vegetables. Select lean meats, poultry (without skin), fish and low-fat dairy products as well.

- Maintain a healthy weight. (See page 8 for a discussion of healthy weights.)

- Exercise regularly. If you have heart disease or haven't exercised lately, check with your doctor first. Start with light to moderate activity at less than 60 percent of maximum heart rate for at least 30 minutes daily.* Suggested activities include walking, swimming, cycling, dancing or gardening. Progress by aiming for vigorous physical activity at 60 percent of maximum heart rate three or more days per week for 20 or more minutes per occasion. Vigorous activities include brisk walking, jogging/running, lap swimming, cycling, skating, rowing and jumping rope.

- Have your blood cholesterol checked if you're over age 20. If it's in the desirable range, have it rechecked every five years (see introduction). If it's too high, work closely with your doctor and registered dietitian to bring it down and keep it down.

Determine maximum heart rate by subtracting your age from 220. For example, if you're 40, your maximum heart rate is 180. Sixty percent of 180 is 108. So when trying to achieve the first activity goal of light to moderate exercise, aim to exercise at an intensity level that gets your heart beating faster but not more than 108 beats per minute.

Cancer

Cancer encompasses more than 100 different diseases, but each is characterized by the uncontrolled growth and spreading of abnormal cells. While you can develop cancer at any age, you're more likely to do so as you age.

Studies show that about 35 percent of cancers may be related to diet. Too much fat in the diet has been associated with cancers of the breast, colon, rectum and prostate, and possibly pancreas, uterus and ovary. A high intake of alcohol has been associated with cancers of the mouth and throat, esophagus, liver, colon, breast, head and neck. Conversely, a diet high in fiber may help reduce risk for cancers of the colon and rectum.

Dietary recommendations to prevent cancer focus on reducing dietary fat and increasing fiber. Guidelines for total fat intake follow those for CHD (page 132). Recommendations for fiber intake range from 20 to 30 grams daily. In addition, it's also advised to avoid obesity and be moderate about alcohol consumption. Finally, the American Cancer Society recommends we limit consumption of smoked, salt-cured and nitrite-cured foods, such as bacon, ham and sausage. Cancers of the esophagus and stomach are common in countries where these foods are eaten in large quantities.

Tips for Reducing Risk of Cancer

- If you smoke, stop.

- Get regular check-ups— once every three years if you're over 20, and every year if you're over 40. Follow your doctor's advice about how often you should be screened for specific cancers.

- Eat a low-fat diet featuring plenty of fiber, whole-grain cereals and breads, fruits and vegetables rich in vitamins C and A, and beta-carotene, such as citrus fruits, red and green peppers, spinach, cantaloupe, peaches, carrots and other dark green or yellow-orange items. Also, eat plenty of cruciferous vegetables such as broccoli, cabbage, cauliflower and Brussels sprouts.

- Limit consumption of salt-cured, smoked and nitrite-cured foods, such as bacon, sausage, ham and frankfurters.

- If you drink alcohol, be moderate—no more than two drinks a day for men and one drink a day for women.

- Maintain a healthy weight. (See page 8 for a discussion of healthy weights.)

- Limit exposure to the sun or artificial sources of ultraviolet light.

Osteoporosis

Osteoporosis is a complex disorder characterized by a progressive loss of bone. While we all lose bone mass as we grow older, a person with osteoporosis loses it at such a rapid rate the bones become fragile and prone to fracture.

Of the many risks that multiply the chances of developing osteoporosis, one of the greatest is being female. Women have smaller and less dense bones to begin with. In addition, women tend to live longer than men, and osteoporosis is a disease that comes with aging.

Menopause seems to be one of the greatest factors that puts women at risk. During menopause, women stop producing the hormone estrogen, which may cause compromised calcium status and result in rapidly accelerated bone loss. Increased calcium in the diet as the single treatment, however, does not seem to be as effective as estrogen-replacement therapy in slowing bone loss after menopause. The risk of developing osteoporosis is greater if you smoke, if you are sedentary and if you do not get enough calcium in your diet.

The recommended daily intake for calcium starts at 800 milligrams per day for children ages one to 11 years. Then it is recommended that through age 24 we consume at least 1,200 milligrams of calcium each day. After that, the recommendation returns to 800 milligrams daily for adults, except for pregnant and breast-feeding women; these women should consume at least 1,200 milligrams of calcium per day. Menopausal or postmenopausal women considered to be at risk for osteoporosis, and who are not undergoing estrogen replacement therapy, may also benefit from a calcium intake of about 1,200 milligrams per day.

Tips for Reducing Risk and Managing Osteoporosis

- Eat a calcium-rich diet, especially during adolescence. Aim for two to three servings daily from the milk, yogurt and cheese group throughout your lifetime.

- Engage regularly in weight-bearing exercises, such as walking or jogging.

- If you smoke, stop.

- If you're menopausal, discuss estrogen-replacement therapy with your doctor.

- Moderate your consumption of alcohol.

Obesity

Although many people associate obesity with excess weight, the term actually refers to an excessive amount of body fat. When a person weighs 20 percent more than is recommended (one of the simplest measures of obesity), he or she is considered to be obese. And obese people run the risk of developing the chronic diseases associated with obesity. According to the U.S. surgeon general, obesity increases risk for diabetes mellitus, high blood pressure and stroke, coronary heart disease, some types of cancer and gallbladder disease.

Although there seems to be a definite genetic component to the tendency for some people to become overweight, lifestyle plays a key role in the development of the condition. In general, Americans tend to eat too much and, very importantly, exercise too little.

Tips for Reducing Risk and Managing Obesity

- Aim for a healthy weight rather than trying to achieve unrealistic goals based on societal standards.

- Eat a balanced, low-fat diet that does not exceed daily caloric requirements and features plenty of whole-grain cereals and breads, fruits and vegetables. Choose low-fat dairy products and lean meat, poultry and fish.

- Eat at least three meals a day to avoid out-of-control hunger.

- Allow yourself to enjoy moderate amounts of high-fat, high-calorie foods, if you want them, to avoid feelings of deprivation that can lead to overeating.

- Exercise regularly, focusing on moderate exercise of greater duration rather than short, intense workouts. Try walking, swimming or cycling.

- Make changes gradually. To avoid overwhelming yourself, first work on improving one or two key habits. When you reach your goals, move on to others you think are important.

Diabetes

People with diabetes have abnormally high levels of blood glucose, the blood sugar that serves as the primary source of energy for the body. Abnormal levels of blood fats, including cholesterol and triglycerides, also commonly accompany the disorder. Diabetes may be caused by a lack of insulin, which is necessary to metabolize the carbohydrate sugar called glucose, by improper functioning of the systems necessary to use insulin properly, or it can be caused by a combination of the two.

There are two major types of diabetes. The onset of Type I diabetes tends to be abrupt and generally occurs before age 30. There is no known means of preventing the disease and we cannot predict who will develop it.

Type II diabetes most commonly develops after age 40 and is often preceded by obesity. Proper diet and exercise help manage Type II, and may help prevent it to the extent that overweight and obesity are avoided. It has long been known that with weight reduction alone, normal blood glucose levels can be reestablished in people with Type II diabetes. In addition, people with Type II diabetes sometimes require insulin to manage the disease, but weight reduction often alleviates that need.

Eating healthfully to prevent Type II diabetes follows the guidelines recommended for reducing risk of obesity (page 134). In addition, dietary guidelines for managing the disease are quite similar: a low-fat diet that features plenty of whole-grain cereals and breads, fruits and vegetables and that does not exceed the calorie levels needed to lose or maintain weight (whichever is necessary for the individual). Concentrated sweets, such as table sugar, candies and honey, should be used sparingly.

Tips for Reducing Risk and Managing Type II Diabetes Mellitus

- Eat a low-fat diet featuring plenty of whole-grain cereals and breads, fruits and vegetables. Enjoy low-fat dairy foods and lean meat, poultry and fish. Limit concentrated sweets such as table sugar, candies and honey.

- Maintain a healthy weight. (See page 8 for a discussion of healthy weights.) If you already have diabetes, check with your doctor to determine what a healthy weight is for you.

- Exercise regularly. If you're sedentary, start with light to moderate physical activity at less than 60 percent of maximum heart rate for at least 30 minutes a day.* Try walking, swimming, cycling, dancing or gardening.

- Develop a management plan with your doctor, if you have diabetes, that includes proper foot care and regular monitoring of your blood glucose and blood fat levels.

*Determine maximum heart rate by subtracting your age from 220. For example, if you're 40, your maximum heart rate is 180. Sixty percent of 180 is 108. So when aiming for light to moderate activity, exercise at an intensity level that gets your heart beating faster but not more than 108 beats per minute.

High Blood Pressure

High blood pressure is defined as blood pressure equal to or greater than 140/90 millimeters of mercury. High blood pressure triples the risk of developing coronary heart disease and increases the risk of stroke by as much as seven times. While the exact cause of the condition is generally unknown, whether you will develop high blood pressure or not seems to depend on a combination of factors. Your chances for developing hypertension are greater if others in your family are affected by the disease, but environmental influences are usually present as well. These influences include obesity, a habitually high alcohol intake (more than two drinks per day), a sedentary lifestyle and various dietary factors.

There has been a great deal of investigation into the impact of sodium on high blood pressure. People with high blood pressure are generally advised to limit their intake of sodium. It's controversial whether people who do not have high blood pressure need to limit sodium. The controversy centers on the concept of sodium sensitivity. It's impossible to tell if you will develop high blood pressure and if you do, whether or not you will be among the sodium sensitive. As a result, many experts suggest most people limit sodium consumption. It's recommended that healthy adults restrict sodium intake to no more than 3,300 milligrams each day.

Tips for Reducing Risk or Managing High Blood Pressure

- Maintain a healthy weight. (See page 8 for a discussion of healthy weights.)

- If you drink alcohol, be moderate—no more than two drinks a day for men and one drink a day for women.

- Exercise regularly.

- Use salt and sodium in moderation. Use salt sparingly in cooking and at the table. Limit consumption of highly salted foods such as chips, pickles and salted nuts. Check labels for the amount of sodium in foods, and choose those lower in sodium when possible.

- Eat a well-balanced, low-fat diet that does not exceed daily caloric requirements and that features plenty of whole-grain breads and cereals, fruits and vegetables. Select low-fat dairy products as well as lean meats, poultry and fish.

- Have your blood pressure checked regularly. If you have high blood pressure, follow your doctor's advice for managing it, and discuss techniques for managing stress such as relaxation.

Managing Food Sensitivities

If you're sensitive to certain foods, you'll probably know it or at least suspect it. You may experience a wide variety of symptoms ranging from skin rashes, hives or asthma to stomach cramps and diarrhea after eating a particular food. Allergies to other substances, such as pollens, animal dander and medications, also may produce some of these symptoms.

Food sensitivities can be divided into several types: true allergies, intolerance to certain foods, gluten sensitivities and idiosyncratic reactions. True allergies trigger the body's immune system, causing it to produce antibodies the first time the food is eaten. When the food is eaten again, negative reactions occur. The most serious of these is anaphylactic shock, a sometimes fatal response that can involve hives, wheezing and fainting. It is generally advised that people with true allergies to specific foods totally avoid those foods. Common foods to which people are allergic include peanuts, eggs, shellfish and cow's milk.

Difficulty with digesting a particular food is called malabsorption or food intolerance, and the most common example may be lactose intolerance. If you're lactose-intolerant, it is because your body doesn't produce lactase, the enzyme necessary to digest lactose, the major carbohydrate in milk. Therefore, when you drink milk, you may develop stomach cramps, pain, diarrhea and/or nausea. Many individuals can consume a small amount of milk (8 ounces or less) without symptoms. Some tolerate milk better if it is consumed with solid foods, such as at mealtime. Some dairy products, such as yogurt with active cultures and aged cheese, contain less lactose than milk and are therefore better tolerated. Some supermarkets now regularly stock lactose-reduced milks for lactose-intolerant people.

Some people are sensitive to gluten, the protein in many grains, including wheat, oats, rye and barley. Gluten sensitivity can result in diarrhea, weight loss and malnutrition, making it a serious condition. If you suspect you are gluten-sensitive, work with your physician or registered dietitian to devise a gluten-free diet. This can be tricky because many foods contain gluten, either as an integral part of the food (such as the wheat in bread) or as part of an additive used in the food.

Idiosyncratic reactions to specific foods or substances occur in some people and can be fatal. One example is asthmatic attacks after ingesting sulfites, which are preservatives used to keep foods from discoloring. Because of such negative reactions, foods that contain sulfites must be so labeled.

Tips for Managing Food Sensitivities

- See your physician to determine whether you're allergic to a specific food. If you find you're truly allergic, avoid the food completely.

- Try drinking milk in small amounts (less than 8 ounces) with solid foods if you're lactose-intolerant. You may also be able to eat yogurt and aged cheeses.

- Work with your physician or registered dietitian to ensure an adequate diet if your child is intolerant to milk. Infants who are diagnosed as allergic to cow's milk usually outgrow the condition by the third or fourth year of life.

- Read labels carefully if you're sensitive to substances such as gluten or sulfites. If you're not sure if a specific product contains an offending substance, contact the manufacturer.

Gastrointestinal Disorders

When we speak of gastrointestinal difficulties, constipation is often the first subject that comes to mind. Chronic constipation is a disorder characterized by small, hard stools that require significant straining to eliminate. It is believed that the condition may lead to the development of varicose veins, hemorrhoids and diverticular disease. In diverticular disease, small herniations (protrusions) form in the colon possibly as a result of increased colonic pressure that arises from constipation.

Eating to help prevent and treat both constipation and diverticular disease focuses on achieving an adequate intake of fiber. Fiber, particularly insoluble fiber such as that found in wheat, increases intestinal bulk and draws water into the intestines. When diverticulitis develops, however, many physicians recommend a reduced-fiber intake until symptoms subside. In addition, stress, fluid intake and exercise levels influence elimination patterns.

Tips for Reducing and Managing Constipation and Diverticular Disease

- Eat a high-fiber diet daily containing at least six servings of breads and cereals, with several of those servings as whole grains and five servings of fruits and vegetables.

- Drink plenty of fluid.

- Exercise regularly.

- Manage stress levels. Discuss relaxation techniques with your doctor.

Nutrition Information

Nutrition Guidelines:

Daily Values are set by the Food and Drug Administration and are based on the needs of most healthy adults. Percent Daily Values are based on an average diet of 2,000 calories per day. Your daily values may be higher or lower depending on your calorie needs.

Recommended intake for a daily diet of 2,000 calories:

Total Fat	Less than 65 g
Saturated Fat	Less than 20g
Cholesterol	Less than 300mg
Sodium	Less than 2,400mg
Total Carbohydrate	300g
Dietary Fiber	25g

Criteria Used for Calculating Nutrition Information:

- The first ingredient is used wherever a choice is given (such as 1/3 cup sour cream or plain yogurt).

- The first ingredient amount is used wherever a range is given (such as 2 to 3 teaspoons milk).

- The first serving number is used wherever a range is given (such as 4 to 6 servings).

- "If desired" ingredients such as "2 tablespoons brown sugar, if desired" and recipe variations are *not* included.

- Only the amount of a marinade of frying oil that is estimated to be absorbed by the food during preparation or cooking calculated.

Cooking Terms Glossary:

Cooking has its own vocabulary just like many other creative activities. Here are some basic cooking terms to use as a handy reference.

Beat: Mix ingredients vigorously with spoon, fork, wire whisk, hand beater or electric mixer until smooth and uniform.

Blend: Mix ingredients with spoon, wire whisk or rubber scraper until very smooth and uniform. A blender, hand blender or food processor can be used.

Boil: Heat liquid until bubbles rise continuously and break on the surface and steam is given off. For rolling boil, the bubbles form rapidly.

Chop: Cut into coarse or fine irregular pieces with a knife, food chopper, blender or food processor.

Crisp-tender: Doneness description of vegetables cooked until tender but still retaining some of the crisp texture of the raw food.

Cube: Cut into squares 1/2 inch or larger.

Dice: Cut into squares smaller than 1/2 inch.

Grate: Cut into tiny particles using small rough holes of grater (citrus peel or chocolate).

Grease: Rub the inside surface of a pan with shortening, using pastry brush, piece of waxed paper or paper towel, to prevent food from sticking during baking (as for some casseroles).

Julienne: Cut into thin, matchlike strips, using knife or food processor (vegetables, fruits, meats).

Mix: Combine ingredients in any way that distributes them evenly.

Sauté: Cook foods in hot oil or margarine over medium-high heat with frequent tossing and turning motion.

Shred: Cut into long thin pieces by rubbing food across the holes of a shredder, as for cheese, or by using a knife to slice very thinly, as for cabbage.

Simmer: Cook in liquid just below the boiling point on top of the stove, usually after reducing heat from a boil. Bubbles will rise slowly and break just below the surface.

Stir: Mix ingredients until uniform consistency. Stir once in a while for stirring occasionally, often for stirring frequently and continuously for stirring constantly.

Toss: Tumble ingredients lightly with a lifting motion (such as green salad), usually to coat evenly or mix with another food.

Ingredients Used in Recipe Testing:

- White rice is used wherever cooked rice is listed in the ingredients, unless otherwise indicated.

- Ingredients used for testing represent those that the majority of consumers use in their homes: large eggs, canned ready-to-use chicken broth, and vegetable oil spread containing *not less than 65% fat.*

- Fat-free, low-fat or low-sodium products are not used, unless otherwise indicated.

- Solid vegetable shortening (not butter, margarine, nonstick cooking sprays or vegetable oil spread as they can cause sticking problems) is used to grease pans, unless otherwise indicated.

Equipment Used in Recipe Testing:

We use equipment for testing that the majority of consumers use in their homes. If a specific piece of equipment (such as a wire whisk) is necessary for recipe success, it will be listed in the recipe.

- Cookware and bakeware *without* nonstick coatings are used, unless otherwise indicated.

- No dark colored, black or insulated bakeware is used.

- When a baking *pan* is specified in a recipe, a *metal* pan was used; a baking *dish* or pie *plate* means oven-proof glass was used.

- An electric hand mixer is used for mixing *only when mixer speeds are specified* in the recipe directions. When a mixer speed is not given, a spoon or fork was used.

Metric Conversion Guide

Volume

U.S. Units	Canadian Metric	Australian Metric
1/4 teaspoon	1 mL	1 ml
1/2 teaspoon	2 mL	2 ml
1 teaspoon	5 mL	5 ml
1 tablespoon	15 mL	20 ml
1/4 cup	50 mL	60 ml
1/3 cup	75 mL	80 ml
1/2 cup	125 mL	125 ml
2/3 cup	150 mL	170 ml
3/4 cup	175 mL	190 ml
1 cup	250 mL	250 ml
1 quart	1 liter	1 liter
1 1/2 quarts	1.5 liters	1.5 liters
2 quarts	2 liters	2 liters
2 1/2 quarts	2.5 liters	2.5 liters
3 quarts	3 liters	3 liters
4 quarts	4 liters	4 liters

Measurements

Inches	Centimeters
1	2.5
2	5.0
3	7.5
4	10.0
5	12.5
6	15.0
7	17.5
8	20.5
9	23.0
10	25.5
11	28.0
12	30.5
13	33.0
14	35.5
15	38.0

Weight

U.S. Units	Canadian Metric	Australian Metric
1 ounce	30 grams	30 grams
2 ounces	55 grams	60 grams
3 ounces	85 grams	90 grams
4 ounces (1/4 pound)	115 grams	125 grams
8 ounces (1/2 pound)	225 grams	225 grams
16 ounces (1 pound)	455 grams	500 grams
1 pound	455 grams	1/2 kilogram

Temperatures

Fahrenheit	Celsius
32°	0°
212°	100°
250°	120°
275°	140°
300°	150°
325°	160°
350°	180°
375°	190°
400°	200°
425°	220°
450°	230°
475°	240°
500°	260°

Note: The recipes in this cookbook have not been developed or tested using metric measures. When converting recipes to metric, some variations in quality may be noted.

Index

Numbers in *italics* refer to photos.